APEX

LEGENDS™

THE OFFICIAL COOKBOOK

THE OFFICIAL COOKBOOK

BY TOM GRIMM &
JORDAN ALSAQA

An Insight Editions Book

CONTENTS

BREAKFAST

APPS & SIDES

SOUPS & STEWS

ENTRÉES

OKONKWO'S

CHICKENBIQUE

STREET MARKET

INDIDI'S SWEETS & DESSERTS

BAKED GOODS

DRINKS FROM THE PARADISE LOUNGE

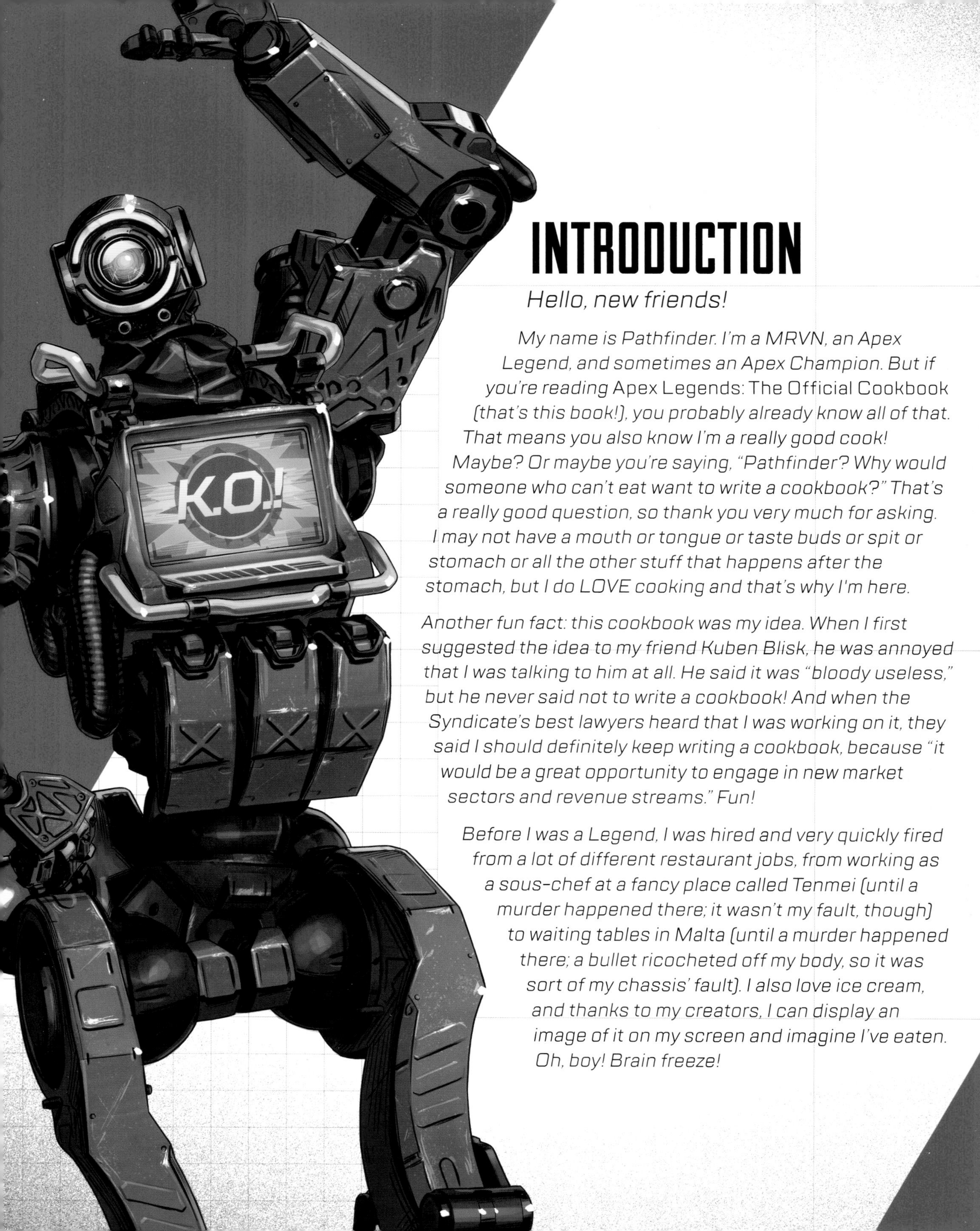

INTRODUCTION

Hello, new friends!

My name is Pathfinder. I'm a MRVN, an Apex Legend, and sometimes an Apex Champion. But if you're reading Apex Legends: The Official Cookbook *(that's this book!), you probably already know all of that. That means you also know I'm a really good cook! Maybe? Or maybe you're saying, "Pathfinder? Why would someone who can't eat want to write a cookbook?" That's a really good question, so thank you very much for asking. I may not have a mouth or tongue or taste buds or spit or stomach or all the other stuff that happens after the stomach, but I do LOVE cooking and that's why I'm here.*

Another fun fact: this cookbook was my idea. When I first suggested the idea to my friend Kuben Blisk, he was annoyed that I was talking to him at all. He said it was "bloody useless," but he never said not to write a cookbook! And when the Syndicate's best lawyers heard that I was working on it, they said I should definitely keep writing a cookbook, because "it would be a great opportunity to engage in new market sectors and revenue streams." Fun!

Before I was a Legend, I was hired and very quickly fired from a lot of different restaurant jobs, from working as a sous-chef at a fancy place called Tenmei (until a murder happened there; it wasn't my fault, though) to waiting tables in Malta (until a murder happened there; a bullet ricocheted off my body, so it was sort of my chassis' fault). I also love ice cream, and thanks to my creators, I can display an image of it on my screen and imagine I've eaten. Oh, boy! Brain freeze!

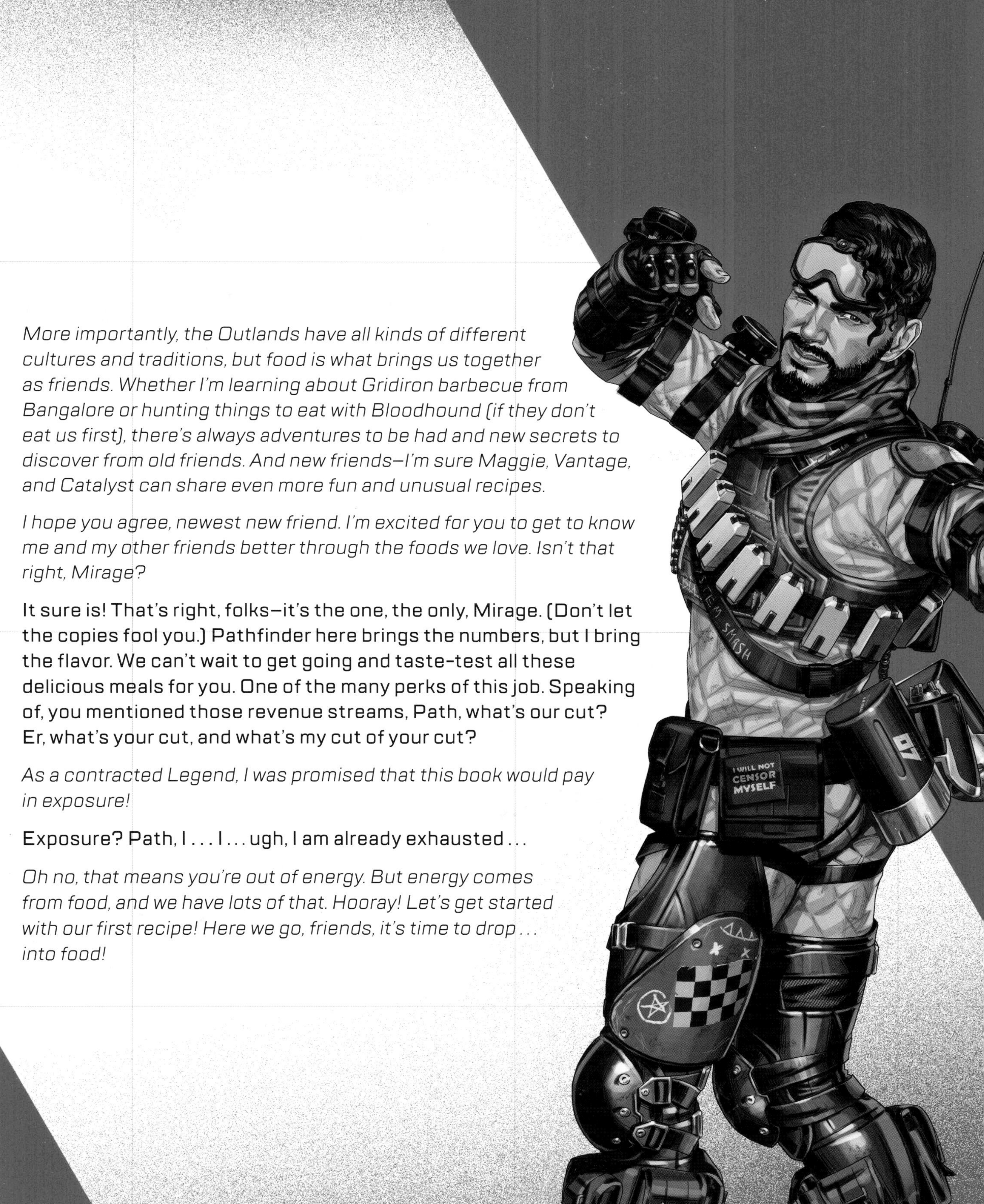

More importantly, the Outlands have all kinds of different cultures and traditions, but food is what brings us together as friends. Whether I'm learning about Gridiron barbecue from Bangalore or hunting things to eat with Bloodhound (if they don't eat us first), there's always adventures to be had and new secrets to discover from old friends. And new friends—I'm sure Maggie, Vantage, and Catalyst can share even more fun and unusual recipes.

I hope you agree, newest new friend. I'm excited for you to get to know me and my other friends better through the foods we love. Isn't that right, Mirage?

It sure is! That's right, folks—it's the one, the only, Mirage. (Don't let the copies fool you.) Pathfinder here brings the numbers, but I bring the flavor. We can't wait to get going and taste-test all these delicious meals for you. One of the many perks of this job. Speaking of, you mentioned those revenue streams, Path, what's our cut? Er, what's your cut, and what's my cut of your cut?

As a contracted Legend, I was promised that this book would pay in exposure!

Exposure? Path, I . . . I . . . ugh, I am already exhausted . . .

Oh no, that means you're out of energy. But energy comes from food, and we have lots of that. Hooray! Let's get started with our first recipe! Here we go, friends, it's time to drop . . . into food!

BREAKFAST

As the first meal of the day, breakfast is the perfect place to start our culinary journey. Just like a Legend landing on the battlefield, it's important to quickly scavenge all you need to make it through the challenges.

These reliable recipes will have you ready for battle before you know it. Let's go, friends, and start our delicious day with a smile!

PATHFINDER'S

POSITIVELY PERFECT PANCAKES

Breakfast is an important start to the day, especially if that day is going to be spent shooting at your very good friends in the arena. Plus, the memory of these fluffy, golden-brown pancakes helps make it easier for them to swallow their eventual defeat! Probably. My friends never say so when I try to feed them on the dropship, but I bet it helps. Make sure to add lots of whipped cream!

Path, you—you got some pancakes left? I mean, I mainly eat the competition for breakfast, but you know, if all that extra powdered sugar and chocolate chips are going to go to waste anyway, I guess I could help you out.

ARTIFICIAL ADVICE

If you want evenly shaped pancakes, you can use a special pancake pan or a mini frying pan to make one pancake at a time.

YIELD
4 SERVINGS

COOK TIME
30 MINS
(including resting time)

DIFFICULTY
SILVER

INGREDIENTS

1¾ cups buttermilk, room temperature
2 eggs, room temperature
2½ cups flour
Pinch of salt
3 teaspoons baking powder
4 tablespoons sugar
1 tablespoon vanilla extract
3 tablespoons butter, plus more for frying (depending on the size of your pan)
Maple syrup
¾ cup fresh berries of choice

PREPARATION

01. In a bowl, use an electric mixer to blend the buttermilk and eggs.

02. In a separate bowl, combine the flour, salt, baking powder, sugar, and vanilla extract.

03. Melt three tablespoons of butter in a small pot over medium heat and add to the dry ingredients with the buttermilk mixture. Gently combine and let stand for 15 minutes.

04. Melt the remaining butter in a large frying pan over high heat and add 3 to 4 tablespoons of batter per pancake, leaving room between the cakes. Cook each pancake on the first side for 2 to 3 minutes until golden brown, then flip. Set on paper towels on a plate to drain, and cover loosely with aluminum foil to keep warm while you prepare the remaining batter.

05. To serve, drizzle generously with syrup and garnish with fresh berries to taste.

REVENANT'S

CEREAL KILLER

Path, why . . . why are these so red? Sure, gotta make it pop but uh . . . these are, like, suspiciously red, you know what I mean? Revenant doesn't eat, right? Too busy with the whole "psychotic murderbot" thing he's got going on? His whole thing is being haunted by hundreds of years of terri . . . tortu . . . very bad things, so why does he remember this recipe? What's it hiding? No, I know you made it, but you said he gave it final approval. Was he ever alone in the room with it? And he calls it what? Buddy, uh, just maybe ask someone else to taste-test, this one for you, 'kay?

YIELD
6 SERVINGS

COOK TIME
15 MINS

DIFFICULTY
SILVER

INGREDIENTS

4¼ cups milk, divided

½ cup sugar

⅝ cup cornstarch

1 egg yolk

Pinch of salt

1 vanilla bean, scraped

½ cup red ringed cereal, such as Froot Loops

1 jar sour cherries, drained

Ready-made cherry sauce, for garnish

PREPARATION

01. Heat 3 cups of milk in a pot over medium heat.

02. Meanwhile, whisk the sugar with the cornstarch and the remaining 1¼ cups of milk in a bowl until smooth. Add the egg yolk and salt, stirring carefully to combine.

03. Remove the pot containing the milk from the heat just before the milk boils. Add the vanilla seeds, pulp, and bean to the pan and allow to stand for 5 minutes. Place back on the heat, bring to a brief boil, and remove the vanilla bean. Slowly stir in the cornstarch mixture, bring the milk to a brief boil again, and turn off the heat.

04. Divide the pudding evenly among 6 small serving bowls. Arrange red ringed cereal around the edge as desired, top the pudding with a few sour cherries, and drizzle generously with cherry sauce.

WRAITH'S
VOIDCRUNCH

My logs show that breakfast is the most important meal of the day, but I guess my friends haven't read them. Some don't eat breakfast at all! Some of them will only eat a bowl of cereal, but at least Wraith makes her Voidcrunch special and nutritious by adding a tasty fruit medley to her oats. She says it "gets the job done" while keeping her light enough on her feet to pierce through the Void whenever she wants. That's very important, because she does it a lot. I use my grappling hook a lot, so maybe I should make a Grapplecrunch for myself.

YIELD
2 SERVINGS

COOK TIME
25 MINS

DIFFICULTY
SILVER

INGREDIENTS

2 tablespoons walnuts, finely chopped

2 tablespoons hazelnuts, finely chopped

4 tablespoons almonds, finely chopped

¼ cinnamon stick, grated

2 tablespoons agave syrup

½ cup old-fashioned rolled oats

1¼ cups oat yogurt

¼ cup frozen blueberries, thawed

1 green apple

PREPARATION

01. Preheat the oven to 350°F. Line a baking sheet with parchment paper.

02. Combine walnuts, hazelnuts, almonds, cinnamon, syrup, and oats in a bowl. Spread an even layer of nut mixture on the baking sheet and bake for 10 minutes or until crisp.

03. Meanwhile, place the oat yogurt and blueberries in a bowl and use an immersion blender to purée smoothly.

04. Wash the apple and pat dry with paper towels. Core the apple and cut into small, thin pieces.

05. Remove the nut-and-oat mixture from the oven and allow to cool for several minutes.

06. To serve, divide the yogurt-blueberry mixture between 2 serving bowls and garnish to taste with the nut-and-oat mixture and apples. Serve immediately.

MIRAGE'S

BAMBOOZLES BREAKFAST CEREAL

When I asked my very best friend Mirage his opinion on breakfast, he agreed that it was very important, thanks to the power of brand recognition! Everyone loves cereal, so if your face is on a cereal box, everyone will love you, too.

That's right, buddy. Athletes have been doing it for centuries, so why wouldn't we Legends get in on the action? The decision's made even easier with these deliscu . . . deliciooo . . . these tasty little sugar clusters, full of flavor that's guaranteed to duplicate with every bite! (Yeah, I came up with that one.) Bamboozles have enough energy in one bowl to fuel six of me at once, so you can be sure they'll keep you going through whatever boring class or morning meeting you've got ahead. Grab a box today before all you're left with is a convincing, but entirely inedible holographic imitation! (Okay, that one might need work.)

YIELD
2 SERVINGS

COOK TIME
5 MINS

DIFFICULTY
BRONZE

INGREDIENTS

1⅓ cups buttermilk
1 tablespoon walnut oil
5 ounces frozen mixed berries, thawed
1 teaspoon maple syrup
Fruit-flavored ringed cereal, for garnish

PREPARATION

01. Pour the buttermilk, walnut oil, frozen berries, and syrup in a blender cup and coarsely purée using an immersion blender.

02. Divide evenly between 2 tall glasses and sprinkle with the cereal.

03. Stir in the cereal just before consuming, and enjoy promptly.

BLOODHOUND'S

BREAK-FEAST

You know, Bloodhound is a Legend of few words, but I'll give 'em this, they know how to put together a breakfast platter. Usually, I'm more of a cereal or cold pizza type of guy; my time's important, I can't be wasting it making breakfast. But hey, if another Legend is helping Path out by making all this food, I mean, somebody's got to eat it, right? And unlike most of these slobs, Bloodhound actually knows the importance of cleaning up after themselves. If only that bird of theirs could be as considerate. Those bar nuts are for paying customers only!

YIELD
4 SERVINGS

COOK TIME
40 MINS

DIFFICULTY
SILVER

INGREDIENTS

Break-Feast Beans
1 tablespoon olive oil
2 onions, diced
2 garlic cloves, minced
1 tablespoon tomato paste
Scant ½ cup vegetable broth
9 ounces canned white beans, drained
5 ounces canned diced tomatoes
Pinch of turbinado or raw sugar
Squeeze of lemon juice
Salt
Cayenne pepper

Scrambled Eggs
4 eggs
8 tablespoons cream
Salt
Freshly ground black pepper
Dried thyme

Fried Eggs
1 tablespoon butter
4 eggs (as fresh as possible)
Salt
Pepper

Break-Feast Sides
4 slices bread
Vegetable oil
8 small tomatoes
8 bratwursts
5 ounces small whole mushrooms
8 slices bacon
Coarse sea salt
Freshly ground black pepper

PREPARATION

To make the break-feast beans:

01. Heat the oil in a frying pan over medium heat. Add the onion and garlic, and sweat until translucent (1 to 2 minutes). Stir in the tomato paste and deglaze with vegetable broth. Reduce for 1 to 2 minutes, then add the beans and tomatoes and stir well to combine. Simmer for 10 minutes, stirring occasionally. Season to taste with the sugar, lemon juice, salt, and cayenne pepper.

To make the scrambled eggs:

02. Crack the eggs into a deep bowl. Add the cream, season generously with salt and pepper, and beat with a wire whisk until still relatively viscous but creamy.

03. Heat a nonstick frying pan over medium heat. Add the eggs to the hot pan and cook slowly until they set, occasionally stirring carefully every 1 to 2 minutes with a pancake turner along the base of the pan so the egg does not burn and stick and instead firms evenly. Once the scrambled eggs have reached the desired consistency, remove from heat and sprinkle with a bit of dried thyme. Season to taste with the sugar, lemon juice, salt, and cayenne pepper. Arrange this hearty warrior's breakfast on large plates with the scrambled eggs, fried eggs, and other tasty treats.

To make the fried eggs:

04. Melt the butter in a nonstick frying pan over medium-high heat. As soon as the butter starts to run and small bubbles form, lower the temperature to medium. Crack open an egg with a short, sharp stroke on the rim of the pan and carefully release into the pan. Leave the egg to cook for 2 minutes, then lower the heat to low and cook through, depending on how hard or runny you like your egg yolk. Remove from the pan and season to taste with salt and pepper. Repeat with the other eggs until you have 4 perfectly fried eggs.

To make the break-feast sides:

05. Heat the oven to about 160°F.

06. Heat a bit of vegetable oil in a nonstick frying pan over medium heat. As soon as the oil sizzles, add the tomatoes, bratwursts, and mushrooms to the pan. Leave the tomatoes alone to cook, but turn the sausages and mushrooms frequently (6 to 8 minutes). Once the food is cooked as desired, set on paper towels on a plate to drain. Cover loosely with aluminum foil and set in the preheated oven to keep warm.

07. Add the bacon to the pan and fry for 1 minute on each side, until crisp. Set on paper towels on a plate to drain.

08. Season the mushrooms with salt and pepper.

09. Toast the bread in a toaster and cut in half diagonally.

10. Arrange this hearty warrior's breakfast with all elements on large plates and serve promptly.

APPS & SIDES

Now that breakfast is done, there are even heartier meals ahead.

Now we're talking! We're getting to the stuff that'll really speak to our fans. Nothing quite complements watching yours truly gun for the win like sharing some delicious finger foods with friends. Really enhances the viewing experience.

I still don't know where on the chicken these fingers come from. I'm excited to learn.

Path, chickens don't actually have . . . You know what, let's just get to the recipes.

VALKYRIE'S

FIERY SANDWICH

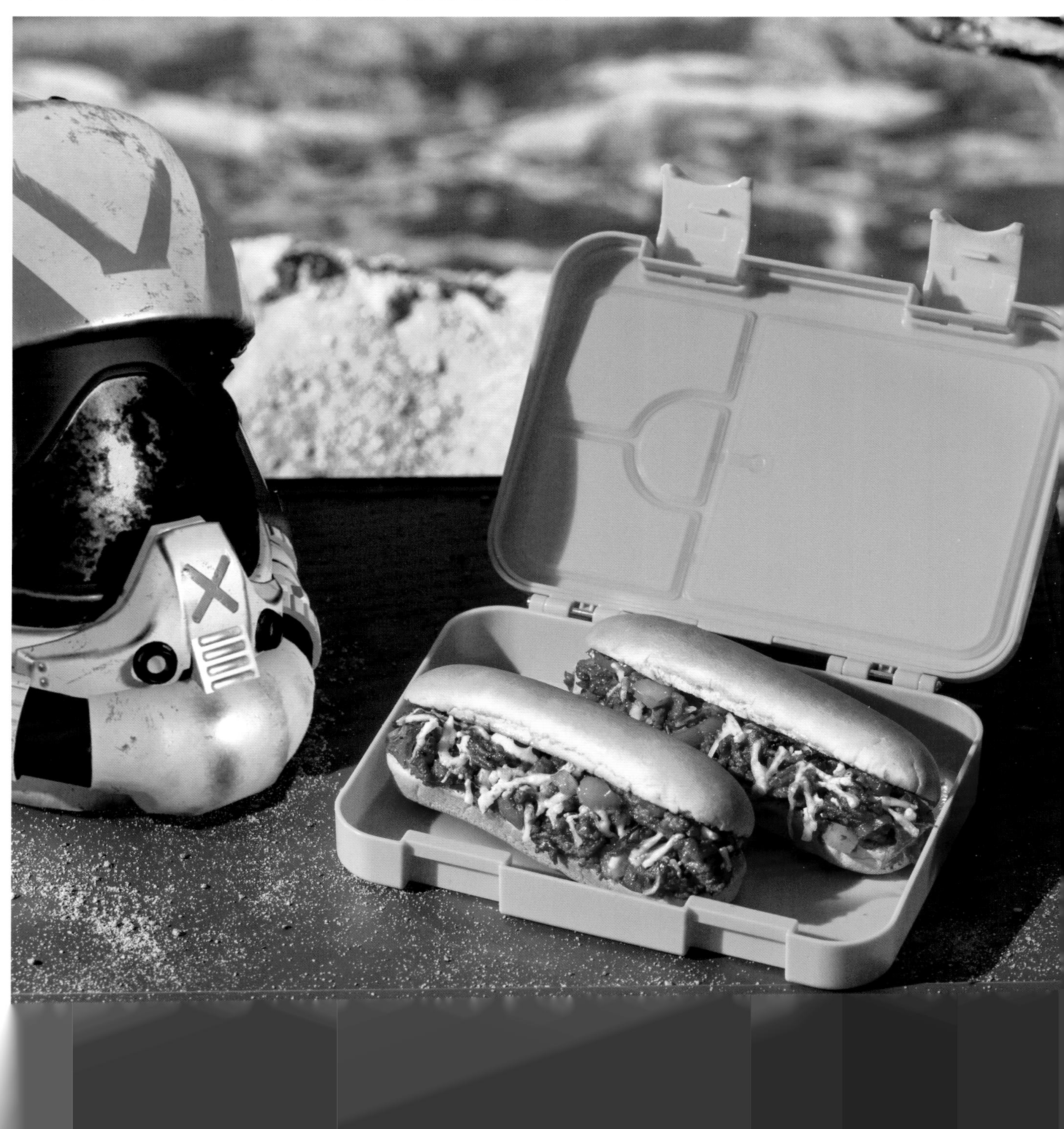

I love my grappling hook because it lets me get to places where I'm not much faster and easier. I believe I would enjoy Valkyrie's jetpack too, but she always says "no" in a very firm tone, which makes me sad. But she still lets me hang on for rides when we're on a team together, and this turns my frown upside down! She even took me to one of her favorite spots in all of Kings Canyon, where she likes to sneak a snack break between fights. And one of her favorite snacks to sneak is this sandwich, and she was happy to share the recipe. Portable, uplifting, and fiery enough to "melt your face right off," just like her jetpack. Oh no, my inability to try it myself has turned my upside-down frown around again!

YIELD
6 SERVINGS

COOK TIME
40 MINS

DIFFICULTY
SILVER

INGREDIENTS

1 tablespoon olive oil
1 shallot, minced
1 garlic clove, minced
¼ cup diced pancetta
1 tablespoon tomato paste
7 ounces ground pork
2 ounces kidney beans
4 ounces canned diced tomatoes
4 ounces mixed vegetables (such as corn, red bell pepper, peas)
Squeeze of lemon juice
1 small red chili pepper, minced
Small pinch of cinnamon
Small pinch of sugar
Salt
Pepper
Paprika
Oregano
Cayenne pepper
6 hot dog buns
2 ounces shredded cheese (such as Mozzarella, Pepper Jack)

PREPARATION

01. Heat oil in a pot over medium heat. Add the shallot and garlic, and sweat until translucent (2 to 3 minutes). Add the pancetta and sear. Stir in the tomato paste and braise for about 1 minute. Add the ground pork, stir well to combine, and cook for 5 minutes, stirring occasionally, until browned on all sides.

02. Add the kidney beans, tomatoes, and vegetables to the pot. Stir well to combine, and simmer, uncovered, for 20 minutes, stirring frequently, so as much liquid as possible evaporates. At the end of the cooking time, add the lemon juice, chili pepper, cinnamon, and sugar. Season to taste with salt, pepper, oregano, paprika, and cayenne pepper. But watch out! It's better to have to add more seasoning later than make it too spicy—even for a fiery warrior like Valkyrie!

03. Toast the hog dog buns in a toaster. Spread a decent serving of the bean-tomato-mixture on the bottom half of each and sprinkle with shredded cheese. (The heat of the chili will melt the cheese.) Carefully press the top half of the bun into place. Set on a large serving plate (or in orange lunch boxes) and enjoy immediately.

VANTAGE'S

BEEF JERKY

Though Xiomara is one of the most recent Legends to join the Games, she quickly became one of my favorite friends to try to eliminate! She was very excited to be part of this project and show me that even though life on Págos can be a harsh trial of survival, that doesn't mean you can't make a delicious snack. On a planet where everything wants to kill you, you have to make sure you kill them first! And since you never know when your next target will show up, it's important to make sure you shoot all of them so you can eat all of them. The curing and marination techniques Vantage taught me can be used on meats from all over the Outlands, not just deadly frozen wastes. And every batch she's made comes with the Echo Seal of Approval; thanks, Echo!

YIELD
ABOUT 12 OUNCES BEEF JERKY

COOK TIME
20+ HOURS
(including marinating and drying time)

DIFFICULTY
SILVER

INGREDIENTS

2 pounds lean beef, such as round or flank steak (less than ¼ inch thick)

8 tablespoons soy sauce

2 tablespoons teriyaki sauce

2 tablespoons Worcestershire sauce

1 tablespoon Tabasco sauce

1 teaspoon garlic powder

1 teaspoon paprika

PREPARATION

01. Rinse the steaks and pat dry with paper towels. Working on a cutting board, cut the steaks across the grain into strips 1¼ to 1½ inches wide. The length of the strips is to your preference.

02. In a small bowl, combine soy sauce, teriyaki sauce, Worcestershire sauce, Tabasco sauce, garlic powder, and paprika.

03. Place the marinade and the steak strips in a freezer bag. Massage the marinade into the meat and marinate in the refrigerator for at least 12 hours (ideally for an entire day).

04. Remove the strips from the marinade and carefully pat dry with paper towels, 1 strip at a time. Arrange the strips on an oven rack so that they do not touch, and place in the oven at 100°F. (Preheating is not necessary.) If your oven does not have such a low temperature setting, set it to the lowest possible temperature and crack the oven door open with the handle of a wooden spoon so the moisture generated inside can escape.

05. Dry the strips of meat in the oven for 4 hours, then turn over and dry for another 3 to 4 hours, or until the jerky has reached the desired consistency. Remove and allow to cool completely.

06. Place in an airtight sealed container and ideally allow to rest for 1 or 2 days before eating so the remaining moisture can spread evenly through the meat. Beef jerky will keep this way for several weeks.

CRYPTO'S

DOSIRAK

Of all my fellow Legends, Crypto has been the hardest to pin down when it comes to favorite recipes. One time, I tried to ask him while he was "down" in a fight, but he didn't like that. Finally, I asked him enough times that he agreed to let me hang out at his workshop and "see what I see." Yay! After an impressive and worrying number of hours without eating a meal, Crypto took this lunch box out of his fridge. He ignored most of my questions, but I was still able to put together all the steps for this recipe by looking over his shoulder. In a way, it was like solving a riddle, and telling each other riddles is something friends do. That makes Crypto a very helpful, very good friend.

YIELD
2 TO 3 SERVINGS

COOK TIME
60 MINS
(plus 3 to 4 weeks to ferment)

DIFFICULTY
GOLD

INGREDIENTS

Kimchi

½ napa cabbage

1 small carrot, peeled and finely grated or julienned

1 bunch green onions, sliced into thin rings

1 small daikon radish, finely grated or julienned

Salt, to taste

2 garlic cloves, coarsely chopped

1 piece fresh ginger root (about 2 inches), coarsely chopped

1 small onion, coarsely chopped

½ sweet apple, finely grated or julienned

2 tablespoons chili powder

2 teaspoons cayenne pepper

1 teaspoon sugar

1 tablespoon fish sauce

Bulgogi

3 tablespoons soy sauce

2 tablespoons sake

1 teaspoon turbinado or raw sugar

Continued on page 30

PREPARATION

To make the kimchi:

01. Use a large, sharp knife to quarter the cabbage, then cut out the core and cut the cabbage into bite-size pieces. Combine with the carrot, green onions, and radish in a large bowl. Add salt to taste. Combine thoroughly and gently knead the salt into the vegetables so they release liquid and stand in their own juices.

02. Use a stand mixer to finely purée the garlic, ginger, onions, apple, chili powder, cayenne pepper, sugar, and fish sauce. If the purée is too thick, add water.

03. Pour the sauce into the bowl containing the vegetables and combine, ensuring that the cabbage is coated with the seasoning on all sides. Layer the kimchi into mason jars that have been rinsed with hot water (or place in freezer bags), pressing down firmly on each layer. Leave about 1¼ inches at the top so the kimchi does not spill over during fermentation. (Important: Make sure the cabbage is fully covered with liquid in the jar and there are no air bubbles in it. Glass fermentation weights are useful for this.) Carefully close the jars and leave at room temperature for 5 to 7 days to ferment. After that, refrigerate for about 2 to 3 weeks, tasting occasionally, until it reaches full flavor.

04. Kimchi will keep, sealed, in the refrigerator for several months.

To make the bulgogi:

05. Combine the soy sauce, sake, sugar, chili powder, garlic, and ginger in a bowl. Add the beef and stir well to combine. Cover loosely with plastic wrap and marinate in the refrigerator for 15 minutes.

06. Once the meat has marinated, heat sesame oil in the frying pan over medium heat. Add the meat, onions, carrot, and spring onions and cook on all sides, stirring occasionally, until the meat is golden brown and the vegetables are done. Sprinkle with toasted sesame seeds to serve.

Continued from page 29

1 teaspoon chili powder

1 garlic clove, finely pressed

1 teaspoon grated ginger root

1 pound beef, very thinly sliced into strips

Sesame oil, for frying (depending on the size of your pan)

1 onion, thinly sliced

1 small carrot, thinly sliced

1 green onion, cut at an angle into about 2-inch pieces

Toasted white sesame seeds, for garnish

Chijimi

1⅔ cups flour

1 cup water

2 eggs

2 teaspoons sesame oil, plus more for frying (depending on the size of your pan)

1 teaspoon salt

1 bunch nira (garlic chives), cut into 2-inch strips

Nira sauce

Chijimi Sauce

3 tablespoons ponzu

2 teaspoons sesame oil

1 teaspoon sugar

1 small green onion, sliced into thin rings

½ teaspoon chili powder

Assembly

Cooked rice, to taste

Additional equipment

Mason jars with lids

To make the chijimi:

07. Combine the flour, water, eggs, oil, and salt in a bowl and use a mixer to work into a very smooth batter with no lumps. Cover the bowl loosely with plastic wrap and refrigerate for at least 3 hours—ideally longer, up to 12 hours—so the flavors can meld.

08. Meanwhile, combine the ingredients for the chijimi sauce in a separate bowl.

09. Add the nira strips to the batter and stir well to combine.

10. Heat some sesame oil on medium heat in a large, nonstick frying pan and pour in ⅓ of the batter. Cover and steam the Korean pancake for 3 minutes. Carefully turn with a pancake turner and cook on the other side for another 3 to 4 minutes, until the chijimi is golden brown. Set on a plate, and follow the same steps with the rest of the batter. To serve, cut into bite-size pieces and drizzle with nira sauce to taste.

To assemble the dish:

11. Neatly arrange the kimchi, bulgogi, and chijimi with cooked rice on the side in a bento box.

THE MOTH AND THE FLAME

Though Catalyst is not a fan of the kitchen, she is a fan of folklore. She told me the story of "The Moth and the Flame" while preparing a dish inspired by the tale. She told me how the moth is drawn to the flame, which I knew right away was a bad thing; moths are not fireproof. As if that wasn't bad enough, the moth also led a blind princess, who it had promised to help, to her doom as well. Oh no! Given the state of the kitchen after Catalyst finished, I wonder if she's the moth, too, and I'm the princess she's led to making another huge mess.

If anyone's the princess, it's me. This place hasn't been clean in weeks, but noooo—somehow, I keep letting you talk me into just one more meal . . .

YIELD
2 SERVINGS

COOK TIME
45 MINS

DIFFICULTY
SILVER

INGREDIENTS

8 jumbo prawns (with shell, without head)

⅛ teaspoon salt

3 slices bacon

1 tablespoon soy sauce

1 teaspoon Worcestershire sauce

2 teaspoons ketchup

¼ teaspoon freshly ground white pepper

½ teaspoon sesame oil

2 tablespoons plus 1 tablespoon vegetable oil

1 egg, beaten

1 garlic clove, minced

2 medium yellow onions, minced

1 tablespoon Shaoxing cooking wine

1 green onion, sliced into fine rings

Additional equipment

Wok (or a large frying pan)

PREPARATION

To butterfly the shrimp:

01. Remove the shells from the shrimp one at a time, leaving only the small segment of shell that connects to the tail. Place the shrimp with the outer convex edge facing down, holding it at the tail with your nondominant hand. Use the tip of your knife to split the tail shell.

02. Starting at the tail and working down, use the pairing knife to cut lengthwise along the inner curve of the shrimp. Don't cut all the way through—leave just enough membrane to keep the symmetrical halves intact. Spread the shrimp out flat on the cutting board and, if needed, press the shrimp lightly into the board to flatten it out further, especially on the tail shell.

03. Carefully scrape away the vein that runs along the edge or through the body of the shrimp.

04. Repeat steps for other shrimp.

To assemble the shrimp:

05. Rinse the shrimp clean under running water. Pat dry with a kitchen towel and return to the cutting board, back side down. Season the shrimp with a light sprinkle of salt. Cut the slices of bacon to match the length of the shrimp. Gently press a bacon strip onto the bottom of each shrimp.

06. Mix the soy sauce, Worcestershire sauce, ketchup, pepper, and sesame oil in a small bowl.

07. Heat the wok over medium-high heat but not to the point of smoking. Add 2 tablespoons of vegetable oil to the wok and swirl to coat it. Dip the shrimp into the beaten egg. Let the excess egg drip off, then place the shrimp in the wok, bacon side down. Work quickly to place all of the shrimp in the wok. Turn up the heat as needed to make sure the egg and bacon cook through.

08. Cook the bacon side of the shrimp for 60 to 90 seconds or until the bacon is golden brown. Carefully use your spatula to turn the shrimp in the same order that you placed them in the pan and cook for another 30 to 60 seconds until the shrimp are cooked through and opaque. Transfer the shrimp to a plate.

09. Heat the wok over medium heat and add the remaining 1 tablespoon of vegetable oil. (Don't wipe down or clean the wok beforehand, so that the oil retains the flavor from frying the shrimp.) Add the garlic and onions and turn the heat up to high. Stir-fry the onions for 30 seconds and add the Shaoxing wine. After another 30 seconds, add the sauce mixture and stir until the onions are coated. Add the green onion.

10. Stir-fry until the onions are done to your liking. Plate the onions and arrange the shrimp on top. Garnish with more green onion and serve.

ASH'S

RAT CHEESE

When I asked Ash if she knew any recipes, she just laughed at me. Not in the friendly way most people do, but the cold, menacing way she laughs at . . . well, everything. The only food she cares about is what she needs for the rat she says is not her pet. I asked the rat what she likes to eat, and Ash gave me a list of special cheeses and told me to go away. I've learned that humans like cheese even more than rats do, so I'm sure they would like to know the favorite cheese of an Apex Legend's non-pet pet rat; I sure did!

YIELD
2 TO 3 SERVINGS

COOK TIME
20 MINS (plus 20 mins for cooling)

DIFFICULTY
SILVER

INGREDIENTS

1⅓ cups flour, plus more for dusting

½ teaspoon salt

3 ounces shredded cheese (such as Pepper Jack, Swiss)

2 tablespoons vegetable oil, plus more for frying (depending on the size of your pan)

⅓ cup milk

PREPARATION

01. Combine flour, salt, and shredded cheese in a small bowl.

02. Add 2 tablespoons of the oil and, working gradually in several batches, the milk. Work in the wet ingredients after each addition. Knead thoroughly until a firm dough forms. Cover with plastic wrap and refrigerate for 20 minutes.

03. Use a rolling pin to roll out the chilled dough as thin as possible on a lightly floured surface. Use a pizza cutter or knife to cut into even squares about 1 inch on a side.

04. Heat 1 inch of vegetable oil in a frying pan over medium heat. Once the oil is hot, add the squares of dough. (Ensure the oil is hot enough that they float.) Fry, stirring occasionally, until golden brown on all sides (about 3 to 4 minutes).

05. Use a slotted spoon or skimmer to remove the cheese snacks from the pan and place on paper towels. Allow to cool for several minutes. Enjoy promptly.

SUPPLY BOX SANDWICH

The Apex Games are designed to go quick, so not everyone eats a good meal before boarding the dropship. But don't worry, this Syndicate-approved lunch box can help even my most malnourished friends stay on their feet—until a bullet makes sure they can't anymore. Be sure to wash it all down with a delicious Shield Cell Soft Drink.

This is a pretty good sandwich. You know what would make it a great sandwich? Making it an official Mirage-branded product. Maybe throw in an advert for the Paradise Lounge? Nothing too big, just an address along the bottom of the container. Who even looks there anyway, right? If anything, I'd be the one taking the loss.

YIELD
4 SERVINGS

COOK TIME
20 MINS

DIFFICULTY
SILVER

INGREDIENTS

1 tablespoon olive oil

12 ounces beef steak, cut into 1-inch-wide strips

Salt

Freshly ground pepper

2 ounces fire-roasted peppers (from a jar), drained

12 slices sandwich bread (such as rye)

5 ounces sun-dried tomato cream cheese

BBQ sauce

2 ounces pickles, drained

4 ounces shredded cheese (such as Mozzarella, Pepper Jack)

Additional equipment

Wraith's Heirloom or wooden skewers (optional)

PREPARATION

01. Heat the oil in a nonstick pan over high heat. Add the beef and sear on all sides, turning occasionally, for about 5 minutes. Season with salt and pepper, then remove and set on paper towels on a plate to drain.

02. Pat the fire-roasted peppers dry and chop until the pieces are bite-size.

03. Preheat the oven's grill or broiler function. Line a baking sheet with parchment paper.

04. Spread an even layer of cream cheese on each bread slice.

05. Place strips of beef on 4 of the slices of bread and drizzle with BBQ sauce to taste. Set another slice of bread neatly on top of each with the cream cheese facing up and arrange a layer of pickles and peppers on top. Drizzle with BBQ sauce and place the last slices of bread on top of each sandwich with the cream cheese facing down. Press lightly to adhere, then sprinkle the top slice of bread generously with shredded cheese.

06. Place the sandwiches on the prepared baking sheet and broil in the oven for about 5 minutes or until the cheese begins to melt. Remove the sandwiches from the oven and give them a bit more oomph with Wraith's Heirloom. (Wooden skewers will also do the job in a pinch.) Serve promptly.

BLOODHOUND'S

BBQ'D FLYER WINGS

This was a fun day! Asking Bloodhound for a recipe led to a whole afternoon of hanging out with my friend in the wilds, but with less than the normal amount of shooting. They explained that to appreciate a recipe, I'd need to hunt down the ingredients myself. I've shot plenty of Flyers in Kings Canyon to stop them from flying away with our loot, but today, the Flyers were the loot! This is what storytellers refer to as "a fun and unexpected twist." After collecting several Flyers, Bloodhound built a fire and taught me exactly how they make a meal outside. You should be able to get the meat you need at a store, but if you want to be like Bloodhound, give your food a fighting chance!

YIELD
4 SERVINGS

COOK TIME
60 MINS (plus 6+ hours to marinate)

DIFFICULTY
SILVER

INGREDIENTS

1 tablespoon dried sage
1 tablespoon dried rosemary
2 tablespoons dried thyme
2 tablespoons paprika
1 tablespoon salt
1 tablespoon cayenne pepper
⅞ cup teriyaki sauce with roasted garlic
½ cup soy sauce
¼ cup buttermilk
2 pounds chicken wings

Additional equipment

Mortar and pestle
1-gallon freezer bag

PREPARATION

01. Add the sage, rosemary, thyme, paprika, salt, cayenne pepper, teriyaki sauce, soy sauce, and buttermilk to a small bowl and stir gently to combine. Pour into a large freezer bag.

02. Rinse the chicken wings briefly, pat dry with paper towels, and place in the bag with the marinade. Seal the bag and refrigerate for at least 6 hours, ideally overnight.

03. Take the wings out of the marinade. Pour the marinade into a small pot and reduce over medium heat, stirring constantly, for 15 minutes, until the marinade is a gleaming dark glaze. Remove from heat and allow to cool slightly.

04. Meanwhile, preheat the oven to 320°F on the convection setting. Position a rack in the middle of the oven. Place a large roasting pan containing about ½ to 1 inch of water underneath the rack to catch any drippings.

05. Brush the wings generously on all sides with the glaze and place them on the rack. Cover loosely with aluminum foil and bake for 40 to 45 minutes, turning every 10 minutes and brushing again with the seasoning mixture. Brush with the remaining glaze, remove the aluminum foil, and increase the oven temperature to 425°F for 5 minutes so the skin gets crispy. Remove and allow to cool for 2 minutes, then serve immediately.

OCTANE'S

FAVORITE FOOD

Keeping up with Octane as he sprints through the city may be more challenging than staying with him on the battlefield. When I asked him what his favorite food is, he took off running all over Solace City to show me. But as soon as he would reach one restaurant, he would change his mind and go sprinting somewhere else. He eventually held still long enough to pick one, but he still couldn't decide between a Tex-Mex burrito and quesadilla as his "favorite favorite" dish. The extreme cheesiness of a quesadilla makes his taste buds sing, but one time he pranked a Silva Pharmaceuticals board member by slipping a firecracker into his lunchtime burrito, so that also has a special place in his heart. I got a list of ingredients for his "favorite favorite" food before he took off again, a burrito in one hand and a quesadilla in the other. I hope his heart doesn't explode.

YIELD
6 SERVINGS

COOK TIME
30 MINS

DIFFICULTY
SILVER

INGREDIENTS

4 tablespoons olive oil
1 pound ground beef and pork blend
2 onions, diced
1 red bell pepper, chopped
1 green bell pepper, chopped
Salt
Pepper
Pinch of cayenne pepper
½ teaspoon ground cumin
1 tablespoon tomato paste
7 ounces canned diced tomatoes
¾ cup canned corn, drained
Pinch of sugar
6 flour tortillas
2 tablespoons crème fraîche or sour cream
6 teaspoons ready-made guacamole
7 ounces shredded cheese (such as Mozzarella, Cheddar)

Additional equipment
Large, shallow baking dish (about 10 by 14 inches)

PREPARATION

01. Heat the olive oil in a frying pan over medium heat and brown the ground meat (about 4 to 5 minutes). Add the onions and peppers and cook the mixture for another 5 minutes. Season generously with salt, pepper, cayenne pepper, and cumin.

02. Stir in the tomato paste and continue to cook briefly (1 minute). Stir in the tomatoes and corn. Cook, uncovered, for several minutes, stirring frequently, until nearly all the liquid has evaporated. Season to taste again with pepper, salt, and sugar.

03. Preheat the oven to 400°F on the convection setting.

04. Spread a layer of sour cream on each of the tortillas, then spread evenly with the ground meat mixture, spread a teaspoon of guacamole on each of them, and sprinkle generously with grated cheese.

05. Roll the tortillas into a burrito shape and set next to each other in the baking dish.

06. Sprinkle with the remaining cheese and bake in the preheated oven for 4 to 5 minutes, until the cheese is melted. Serve immediately.

PÃO DE QUEIJO

Loba and I had a great time pulling off a heist today! She wanted to share one of her favorite foods with me, but the only vendor who sells these cheesy rolls in Solace City has given her a lifetime ban. Apparently, something Loba did convinced him she's a conwoman, which is true, but I've been conned by Loba and that worked out mostly great for me! While I distracted the shopkeeper, Loba teleported in and grabbed a bag of this snack. Now, Loba says any time she wants pão de queijo, I'm her go-to guy. I did still go back and pay the vendor, though; I've accidentally become a wanted outlaw enough times to know I don't want to become one again on purpose.

YIELD
ABOUT 20 CHEESE BUNS

COOK TIME
30 MINS

DIFFICULTY
SILVER

INGREDIENTS

½ cup water

½ cup milk, divided

¼ cup butter

1 teaspoon salt

3½ cups tapioca flour

2 eggs

7 ounces shredded cheese, as sharp and full flavored as possible (ideally, Swiss or Parmesan)

Additional equipment

Ice cream scoop (about 2 inches in diameter, optional)

PREPARATION

01. Preheat the oven to 350°F on the convection setting. Line a baking sheet with parchment paper.

02. Bring the water, ¼ cup of milk, butter, and salt to a boil in a small pot over medium heat, stirring occasionally. Remove from heat. Add the tapioca flour to the liquid and stir briefly with a wooden spoon. Add the eggs and the remaining ¼ cup of milk and knead thoroughly by hand. Add the cheese and carefully knead until all ingredients are combined into a compact, slightly sticky dough.

03. Use an ice cream scoop to shape the dough into bite-size balls. Set the balls on the prepared baking sheet, about 1 inch apart, and bake for about 20 to 25 minutes or until the balls are crisp on the outside and soft and chewy inside. Remove from the oven and allow to cool on the baking sheet for several minutes.

04. These are best served fresh from the oven with butter, salt, and a cold beverage, such as Wraith's Appletini (Page 152).

SOUPS & STEWS

Mirage, what's the difference between a soup and a stew?

Huh. Well, stews, uh . . . have more chunks? So, I guess if you added some chunky stuff, a soup would become a stew?

Chicken soup has chunks of chicken, and it's not a stew.

Okay, how about the viss . . . viscosis . . . the thickness? Stews tend to be a lot thicker.

That's true. But what about chowder?

Path, you're making this more complicated than it needs to be.

SEER'S

BANGA SOUP

The planets and cultures that make up the Outlands are very interesting, and so many of my friends take pride in sharing their home planet's unique traditions. For example, Seer loves Boreas and the foods that are common there, like this palm nut soup dish that he ate when he was a child. It can be difficult to get children to eat nutritious foods, so the taste of this dish must really be off the charts! I'll have to remember that when I find my child—even if he doesn't eat, I bet it will be helpful somehow.

ARTIFICIAL ADVICE

This Nigerian dish is traditionally made with tripe (shaki), cow skin (ponmo), and cow foot. It has been modified with ingredients that may be easier to find, but feel free to swap them back.

YIELD
6 SERVINGS

COOK TIME
60 MINS

DIFFICULTY
SILVER

INGREDIENTS

1 tablespoon vegetable oil
1 small onion, diced
2 pounds stew beef
7 ounces stockfish (such as dried cod), torn into small pieces
4 ounces dried prawns
1 quart (32 fluid ounces) beef stock
2 cubes beef bouillon
3½ cups palm nut concentrate
7 cups water
2 to 3 Scotch bonnet chilis, puréed
Edible periwinkle, finely chopped (optional)
1 tablespoon banga seasoning
1 banga (oburunbebe) stick
6 medium fresh wolffish steaks (ready to cook)
7 ounces frozen prawns, thawed
1 to 2 tablespoons beletete leaf, finely chopped
Salt and pepper

PREPARATION

01. Heat the oil in a large pot over medium heat and sauté the onions until translucent (2 to 3 minutes). Add the stew beef and cook for 3 minutes, until brown on all sides. Add the dried fish and prawns, stir well to combine, and pour in the broth. Add the bouillon cubes and simmer, stirring occasionally, for 45 minutes or until the meat is tender.

02. Meanwhile, pour the palm nut concentrate and water in a medium-size pot. Stir well to combine, then simmer, uncovered, for 20 minutes. Once the liquid has thickened noticeably and oil begins to form on the surface, add the puréed chilis, periwinkle (if desired), banga seasoning, and oburunbebe stick and simmer for 10 minutes, stirring occasionally. Add the mixture to the pot containing the meat.

03. Add the fresh fish, prawns, and beletete leaf to the pot and simmer over low heat for 10 to 12 minutes. Do not stir, or the fish will fall apart. Season to taste with salt and pepper.

CUP O' SOUP

My good friend Nat–that is my nickname for Wattson–is very inspiring. Even though she lost her father, she never gave up on all the things they loved doing together. She is always experimenting with electricity and helping others deal with crises—which happen a lot around here! In the kitchen, it means experimenting with recipes, trying to find the perfect mix of flavors, and this tasty soup is the result. She said it will "give you a jolt," and then laughed. Oh! I get it.

Yeah, eating lightning is bad for most of us, bud. Soup's good, though! One cup is not nearly enough. I'm thinking we go for a full Gallon O'Soup in the future. Actually, scratch that, I haven't been paid a consulting fee, so stick with the name you've got.

Sluuurrrrrppp.

YIELD
4 SERVINGS

COOK TIME
45 MINS

DIFFICULTY
SILVER

INGREDIENTS

1 teaspoon olive oil

3 onions, diced

1 pound combined soup vegetables (such as carrots, celery, leek, parsley), diced

2 teaspoons tomato paste

14-ounce can diced tomatoes

14-ounce can white beans

5 ounces canned kidney beans

1 quart vegetable broth

2 salami sausages, sliced

Salt, to taste

Marjoram, to taste

Paprika, to taste

Chopped fresh parsley, for garnish

PREPARATION

01. Heat the oil in a medium pot over medium heat. As soon as the oil is hot, add the onions, and sweat until translucent (2 to 3 minutes). Add the vegetables and sauté vigorously for 3 to 4 minutes on all sides. Stir in the tomato paste and braise briefly (1 minute).

02. Add the tomatoes, white beans, and kidney beans to the pot and stir frequently. Add the sausage and simmer for 5 minutes more.

03. Season to taste with salt, marjoram, and paprika. To serve, sprinkle with chopped fresh parsley.

OCTANE'S

POWER BOWL

Oh, man, note to self, make better life choices. I mean, I'm the party guy, but Octane . . .? That guy's a live wire in a human body. I think if he slows down, he explodes or something. Oof, we made a mess of the place. Or was that Path and another one of his cooking buddies? Well, Octane left me a pick-me-up, at least. "Octane's Powershot," huh? What am I even looking at? Is this another drink? One of his stims? Heck, could be a soup, as warm as it is. Or a stew? Soup and stew, what's the difference? Whatever. Point is, I'm not drinking this. Definitely not.

. . . Ugh, where's a bowl?

YIELD
4 SERVINGS

COOK TIME
4+ HOURS

DIFFICULTY
SILVER

ARTIFICIAL ADVICE
Chop the beef into small pieces and add it to the broth, or use it to prepare other dishes.

INGREDIENTS

2 onions

1 bouquet garni (made from herbs such as lovage, parsley, thyme, rosemary, sage; 2 twigs each)

4 marrow bones

1 pound combined soup vegetables (such as carrots, celery, leek, parsley), coarsely chopped

2 garlic cloves

5 peppercorns

2 to 3 bay leaves

2 whole allspice berries

5 juniper berries

1 whole clove

1 tablespoon marjoram

2 pounds beef brisket (or other cut of beef)

Pinch of salt

Chives, freshly chopped, for garnish

Additional equipment

Kitchen twine

Cheesecloth (optional)

PREPARATION

01. Cut onions in half without peeling. Heat a frying pan over medium heat and place the half onions in the pan, cut side down. Sear for 2 to 3 minutes (without oil).

02. Use kitchen twine to bunch the fresh herbs together into a bouquet garni.

03. Wash the marrow bones and place them in a large soup pot. Add the vegetables, onion, garlic, bouquet garni, peppercorns, bay leaves, allspice, juniper, clove, marjoram, and meat. Season with salt.

04. Fill the pot with cold water until all ingredients are covered and bring to a gentle boil, cooking over medium heat for 20 minutes. Raise the heat to medium-high and keep at a rolling boil for 40 minutes. Lower the heat to medium and simmer, uncovered, for 3 hours, stirring occasionally.

05. Line a fine strainer or sieve with cheesecloth (or 2 layers of paper towels) and pass the soup through it into a clean pot. To serve, sprinkle with chives.

PATHFINDER'S

NEW EASTERN LEVIATHAN STEW

Every friend I've told about this cookbook has raised their eyebrows (those that have eyebrows, anyway). I've been fired from lots of restaurants for breaking things, injuring patrons, setting fires, and having accidental deaths happen near me. It's funny how those are good things in the Games, but very bad things in food service. However, thanks to my passion for recipes and a can-do attitude Mirage calls "trying on the best days," I was always able to find more work. Yay for all my trying! And no recipe has been more helpful than the one for Leviathan Stew. It even got me a job at Tenmei, one of Psamathe's most acclaimed restaurants. I was fired from there, too, but now I can make this dish for all my new friends!

YIELD
4 SERVINGS

COOK TIME
50 MINS (plus 2 to 3 hours for stewing)

DIFFICULTY
SILVER

INGREDIENTS

2 to 3 tablespoons clarified butter (ghee)

2 cups onions, diced

2 garlic cloves, minced

2 tablespoons tomato paste

2 to 3 tablespoons white wine vinegar

2 tablespoons paprika

3 cups beef stock

2 bay leaves

2 pounds beef (shank or shoulder), coarsely cubed

10 potatoes (floury), cut into slices

½ red bell pepper, cut into thin strips

½ green bell pepper, cut into thin strips

Salt

Freshly ground pepper

Additional equipment

Large Dutch oven or other heavy-bottomed, oven-safe pan with lid

PREPARATION

01. Melt the clarified butter over medium heat in a large Dutch oven or other heavy-bottomed, oven-safe pan. Add the onions and sauté until translucent (2 to 3 minutes). Add the garlic and sweat. Cook, stirring occasionally, for 5 to 8 minutes, until the onions are golden brown.

02. Preheat the oven to 350°F on the convection setting.

03. Combine the tomato paste, vinegar, and paprika in a bowl. Add the beef stock and combine to make a smooth, slightly runny paste. Pour over the onion mixture in the pan and stir to combine. Add the meat, potatoes, red and green bell pepper, and bay leaves. Make sure that everything is covered with liquid. If necessary, top up with water.

04. Cover the pan and place on the middle oven rack. Stew for 2 to 3 hours, stirring occasionally to combine. Remove the bay leaves, season to taste with salt and pepper, and serve.

VALKYRIE'S

CURRY BEEF UDON COMBO

Valkyrie used to live near Angel City, which is very far away. She said she didn't have fresh food on the trip, so she was pulling her hair out after eating so much "freeze-dried cardboard." She made a dish like this while she was traveling, using beef jerky and canned vegetables, but when she found her new home on Gaea, she made this with the juiciest pieces of beef she could buy. This combo dish mixes Gaean and Angelian cuisine to create a unique noodle dish that promises a missile swarm to the taste buds—which she says is a good thing.

YIELD
4 SERVINGS

COOK TIME
30 MINS

DIFFICULTY
SILVER

INGREDIENTS

Sesame oil, for frying (depending on the size of your pot)

8 ounces beef, thinly sliced into strips

1 tablespoon soy sauce, plus more to taste

1 tablespoon sake

4 tablespoons yellow curry paste

1 quart dashi (instant, mixed according to the instructions on the package)

20 pearl onions (from a jar), drained

¼ cup canned corn, drained

¼ yellow bell pepper, minced

¼ green bell pepper, minced

1 small red chili pepper, sliced into thin rings

8 ounces udon noodles

Salt

1 tablespoon cornstarch (optional)

¼ cup water (optional)

1 green onion, sliced into thin rings

Black sesame, for garnish

White sesame, for garnish

PREPARATION

01. Heat oil in a medium pot over high heat. Add the beef strips and brown on all sides for about 3 to 4 minutes. Deglaze with soy sauce and sake. Reduce briefly, then stir in the curry paste and pour the dashi over it.

02. Add the pearl onions, corn, bell peppers, and chili peppers to the pot. Stir well to combine and simmer, uncovered, for 10 minutes, stirring occasionally.

03. Meanwhile, cook the udon noodles in generously salted water according to the package directions, then drain in a strainer.

04. Once the meat is done and the vegetables are tender, check the consistency of the soup. It should be thick. If necessary, dissolve 1 tablespoon of cornstarch in ¼ cup of water, stir into the contents of the pot, and bring to a brief boil to reach the desired consistency. Add the noodles.

05. Season to taste with soy sauce (optional), stir in the green onion, and sprinkle with black and white sesame for garnish.

MAD MAGGIE'S

MĀORI BOIL UP

Some of my friends can get very creative in the kitchen. After I asked the Syndicate to let Maggie out of jail for a while so she could help me with this cookbook, she and I—along with several heavily armed guards—spent several hours preparing the ingredients for this dish out in the wild. She said it wasn't even close to a full Salvonian Feast, but it would do. But then we found out our burner was out of gas. Oh no! Instead of giving up, Maggie used her Riot Drill on the lid. The pot got so hot that everything boiled right up. She destroyed the pot lid though, so you should use a well-fueled stove for this recipe–or a lot of pots.

Uh, just to check, is any of the cookware I lent you going to make it back in one piece, or should I just . . . nevermind. What's the point of an armed escort if she's just going to destroy my stuff, anyway.

YIELD
5 TO 6 SERVINGS

COOK TIME
ABOUT 2 HOURS

DIFFICULTY
SILVER

INGREDIENTS

1 pound spare ribs

1 knuckle (hock) of pork (about 2 pounds)

2 large onions, diced

Salt

Freshly ground black pepper

1 cup flour

2 tablespoons baking powder

4 tablespoons water

3 medium potatoes, cubed

2 large sweet potatoes, cubed

½ winter squash, cubed

1 bunch watercress, coarsely chopped

PREPARATION

01. Place the ribs in a large pot and add water to cover. Bring to a boil over medium heat and simmer for 5 minutes, then pour off the liquid.

02. Add the pork knuckle and onions to the pot and add water to cover all. Season to taste with salt and pepper, bring to a boil, and simmer for 90 minutes, stirring occasionally.

03. Meanwhile, combine the flour and baking powder with 4 tablespoons of water in a small bowl until the ingredients form a dough. Using slightly moistened hands, shape the dough into balls the size of golf balls.

04. Remove the ribs from the pot and set aside. Add the potatoes, sweet potatoes, and squash, stir well to combine, and simmer for 5 minutes. Add the balls of dough and simmer for another 10 minutes.

05. Add the ribs and watercress and cook for another 5 minutes, until the watercress is soft. Season to taste again with salt and pepper.

WATTSON'S

EELHEAD STEW

When Wattson told me about this dish, she said we'd need to source our main ingredient locally. It seems my grasp on sarcasm has not advanced as far as I thought, because when I asked if that meant getting them directly from the bay ourselves, I took her thumbs-up and wink literally. Imagine my surprise when after many hours of trying to fish for eels down at the docks, I returned to Wattson's workshop and found she'd already purchased all of the ingredients at the market. I still think my ingredients were fresher, but on the plus side, I now have several new slippery friends!

ARTIFICIAL ADVICE

Instead of filleting the smoked eels, you can chop them into bite-size pieces and cook them that way. That will save you some time preparing the dish, but watch out for bones!

YIELD
4 SERVINGS

COOK TIME
60 MINS

DIFFICULTY
GOLD

INGREDIENTS

2 smoked eels, ready to cook

2 tablespoons butter, divided

About 1 pound soup vegetables (such as carrots, leek, celery, parsley, parsnips), coarsely chopped

Scant ½ cup dry white wine

1⅔ cups vegetable broth

2 onions, diced

2 potatoes, cut into about ¼-inch cubes

About 5 ounces mixed dried seedless fruit (such as plums, apricots, peaches, apples)

½ cup frozen peas

½ small red chili pepper, minced

Salt

Pepper

Chopped fresh dill, for garnish (optional)

PREPARATION

01. Place an eel on a large cutting board. Cut off the head and slice the skin open lengthwise, first folding it out and then carefully removing it. Using a small, sharp knife, carefully scratch off the small black scraps of skin that remain on the outside of the fish. Cut the eel in half horizontally and use your fingers to carefully remove the eel fillets from the head side. Carefully double-check the eel fillets for any bones, then cut into bite-size pieces. Set the skin, head, and bones aside. Repeat for the other eel.

02. Place 1 tablespoon butter in a large pot and melt over medium heat. Add ¼ of the vegetables and sauté vigorously on all sides for 6 to 7 minutes. Deglaze with white wine, then add the vegetable broth. Add the skin, heads, and bones to the broth and simmer for 15 minutes, stirring occasionally.

03. Meanwhile, melt 1 tablespoon butter in a medium-size pot over medium heat and add the onions, the potatoes, and the remaining ¾ of the vegetables. Let the contents sweat for a few minutes.

04. Pour the smoked eel broth through a fine sieve into the pot with the vegetables and bring to a boil. Add the dried fruit, peas, and chili pepper and simmer for 10 minutes or until the vegetables are cooked. Season to taste with salt and pepper. To serve, sprinkle with dill if desired.

VALKYRIE'S

LEVIATHAN UDON

Valkyrie learned this recipe from her mother. She says her mom was always happy to teach her anything she could. Apparently, this was the exact opposite of her father, who never let her even think about learning how to pilot a Titan like he did. She insists she is not bitter about this fact, though she is the one who brought it up. Of course, when I pointed that out, she asked if I wanted to learn the recipe or not. As I very much did, I stopped asking questions about the things I never asked about in the first place.

Just because you're cooking with leviathan doesn't mean you need to use such big cuts of meat, yeesh. It barely fits in the bowl! And do not make a "big mouth" joke.

YIELD
2 SERVINGS

COOK TIME
45 MINS

DIFFICULTY
SILVER

INGREDIENTS

Ajitsuke Tamago

Ice cubes
2 eggs
2 tablespoons soy sauce
2 tablespoons mirin
6 tablespoons water

Wakame Salad

5 teaspoons white sesame seeds
4 ounces fresh wakame seaweed
1 teaspoon lime juice
½ teaspoon rice syrup
1 tablespoon sesame oil
Freshly ground black pepper

Udon Noodles

7 ounces udon noodles
Salt

Additional Ingredients

1 nori sheet
1 quart (32 fluid ounces) chicken stock
2 tablespoons sake
1 tablespoon soy sauce
4 ounces canned edamame, drained
1 small red chili, sliced into thin rings
Narutomaki, sliced
½ bunch green onions, sliced into thin rings
1 carrot, peeled and julienned
Furikake seasoning

PREPARATION

To make the ajitsuke tamago:

01. Place some ice cubes in a bowl of cold water.

02. Carefully set the eggs in a small pot with water to cover. Bring to a boil over medium heat and cook for 7 minutes. Use a skimmer or slotted spoon to remove the eggs from the pot and immediately plunge them into the ice water.

03. While the eggs are cooling, combine the soy sauce, mirin, and water in a bowl, then pour mixture into a small freezer bag.

04. Carefully shell the chilled eggs and add them to the marinade in the freezer bag. Seal the bag so that the eggs are covered on all sides with marinade, and refrigerate for at least 12 hours (and up to 3 days).

05. Cut the marinated eggs in half horizontally.

To make the wakame salad:

06. Heat a frying pan over medium heat. Add the sesame seeds and toast for 3 minutes. Remove, transfer to a small bowl, and allow to cool.

07. Wash the wakame and drain in a strainer. Transfer to a bowl, add the lime juice, syrup, and oil, and combine well. Season with pepper to taste. Add the toasted sesame and combine. Cover the bowl with plastic wrap and refrigerate until ready to use.

To make the udon noodles:

08. Cook the udon noodles according to the instructions on the package in generously salted water and drain in a strainer.

To assemble the dish:

09. Use kitchen shears to cut the nori sheet into 8 squares of equal size.

10. Heat the chicken stock, sake, and soy sauce in a pot over medium heat. Add the edamame and red chili and simmer for 10 minutes.

11. Once all of the components of the dish are done, divide the udon noodles among 4 large serving bowls. Place the noodles in the middle of each and arrange the nori sheets, the narutomaki slices, half a ramen egg, the onions, the wakame salad, and the julienned carrots around them. Add broth to taste, then sprinkle with toasted sesame and furikake seasoning as desired and serve immediately.

LIFELINE'S

CARE PACKAGE

You know what's great advice? Don't piss off your healer. Common sense, right? If your teammate with the high-tech medical robot is mad at you, maybe they take a little longer than necessary to patch you up. Well, turns out that advice still applies off the battlefield, too. You make one too many jokes about Lifeline skimping out on the potluck and before you know it, she's got her drop pod crashing through the roof of your bar just to spite you! Sure, it came fully loaded with a bunch more snacks, which people appreciated, but my roof! Who's even up there loading food into those things, anyway?

ARTIFICIAL ADVICE

You can also prepare this stew with a soup hen instead of a broiler, but less fat will remove some of the soup's richness. Also, remember that soups and stews often taste even better the next day.

YIELD
6 SERVINGS

COOK TIME
90 MINS

DIFFICULTY
SILVER

INGREDIENTS

1 tablespoon oil

1 onion, diced

1 pound combined carrots, celery, leek, parsley, diced

1 ready-to-cook broiler chicken (about 2½ pounds)

2 bay leaves

5 juniper berries

5 black peppercorns

1 tablespoon salt, plus more to taste

1 quart chicken stock

6 chicken legs

2 cups uncooked pasta of your choice

1 cup frozen peas

Pepper

Some fresh parsley, for garnish

PREPARATION

01. Heat the oil in a large soup pot over medium heat. Once the oil is hot, add the onions, and sweat until translucent (2 to 3 minutes). Add the chopped vegetables and sauté for 5 to 6 minutes, until browned on all sides.

02. Add the broiler chicken, bay leaves, juniper berries, peppercorns, and 1 tablespoon of salt to the pot. Stir briefly to combine, and deglaze with the stock. Add enough water to cover the chicken completely and simmer, uncovered, for 30 minutes. Add the chicken legs and simmer for another 30 minutes.

03. Use a skimmer or slotted spoon to carefully remove the cooked chicken from the pot and set it on a deep plate. Allow to cool to the point that you can pick off the meat without burning your fingers. While the chicken is cooling, prepare the pasta of your choice in a separate pot, following the directions on the package. Do not cook the pasta beyond al dente (firm to the bite), since the pasta will continue to cook after being added to the hot soup and might otherwise get mushy. Drain the pasta and set aside.

04. Pull the meat off the cooled chicken carcass and tear into bite-size pieces. Remove the legs from the soup and set aside. Strain the chicken broth into a clean, large pot, removing desired vegetables from the strainer and adding them back to the pot. Add the peas and chicken and reheat over low heat for several minutes. Season to taste with salt and pepper immediately before serving.

05. To serve, place some of the noodles in a shallow soup bowl and fill with soup. Garnish each serving with fresh parsley and a chicken leg.

ENTRÉES

All right, on to the main course! You know, this cookbook felt like it was going to take a long time, but it's really flown by. I'm going to miss working on this thing with you, Path.

No worries, friend, we're not even halfway done yet!

Not halfway... We're at the entrées! Slap a few desserts on the end, throw in a table of contents and a heartfelt dedication to your best bud Mirage, bingo bango, we're done!

We will definitely add desserts, but we also have restaurants to learn about in the "specialty sections."

Hmm, I do like a good restaurant. All right... but you're treating!

MIRAGE'S

GLAZED PORK CHOPS

Here we go, folks: the recipe that started it all. My illustrious cooking career, I mean. See, Path, I told you. All you've got to do to get someone reclu . . . reluctin . . . reluctav . . . unwilling to take part in our little cooking extravaganza is to turn it into a cook-off! Nobody who makes it to Legend status does it without a competitive streak. Seriously, look how excited they all are to get beat by Great Grandpa Gryz's pork chops. Behemoth or not, Bloodhound, a burger's not going to cut it! Fuse, Maggie, you really think Salvonian cooking's going to win over this crowd? And things are looking a little smoky over there, Bangalore, hope you aren't burning it! Actually . . . what's that smell . . . Uh, I probably should focus on my chops, heh.

ARTIFICIAL ADVICE

If you want to cook the meat on the grill, preheat your grill as usual. Dab the chops with kitchen towels to remove as much marinade as possible, and grill for 3 to 4 minutes on each side. Then remove from the grill and let rest, loosely covered with aluminum foil, for 5 minutes before eating.

YIELD
4 SERVINGS

COOK TIME
45 MINS
(including marinating time)

DIFFICULTY
SILVER

INGREDIENTS

1 tablespoon olive oil

5 ounces balsamic vinegar

2 tablespoons turbinado or raw sugar

2 teaspoons Dijon mustard

1½ tablespoons garlic, minced

1 teaspoon smoked paprika

Pinch of salt

Pinch of pepper

Scant ½ cup Witt's Whiskey (optional) (Page 170)

4 pork chops

1 tablespoon butter

PREPARATION

01. In a bowl, combine the oil, vinegar, sugar, mustard, garlic, paprika, salt, pepper, and, if desired, a solid slug of Witt's Whiskey. Pour into a large freezer bag and add the pork chops. Seal the bag and massage the marinade vigorously into the meat. Refrigerate for at least 30 minutes to marinate. Longer is welcome (up to 8 hours)!

02. Melt the butter in a large frying pan over high heat. Remove the pork chops from the marinade and add them to the hot pan, browning 2 to 3 minutes each on each side, until the meat is slightly brown. Add the marinade to the pan and cook for another 3 minutes, brushing the meat with the marinade on all sides.

03. Remove the pork chops from the pan and serve to taste with the thickened marinade as sauce. Excellent with Golden Chips (Page 104) or Potato Wedges (Page 103).

BIG BANG PIZZA

Some mornings you wake up too late or too tired or too hungover from a night of partying just a bit too hard on your party ship to want to put in the effort, y'know? You need something that takes minimal effort to prepare, and what's less effort than ordering a pizza? I know a guy who knows a guy at Big Bang corporate, and they were willing to sponsor a whole full-page ad for their new delivery app, but Path said that "would not be in the spirit of a cookbook" or whatever. So, next-best thing, here's how they make their pies. You, uh... you didn't get this from me, though.

YIELD
2 PIZZAS

COOK TIME
30 MINS

DIFFICULTY
SILVER

INGREDIENTS

1 tablespoon olive oil
1 shallot, minced
1 garlic clove, pressed
9 ounces canned diced tomatoes
¼ teaspoon balsamic vinegar
Salt
Pepper
2 tablespoons Italian seasoning
1 pound ready-made pizza dough
Flour, for dusting
¼ red bell pepper, diced
¼ yellow bell pepper, diced
¼ green bell pepper, diced
2 to 3 mushrooms, thinly sliced
1 tomato, thinly sliced
3 to 4 canned black olives, thinly sliced
5 ounces ready-to-eat chicken pieces
4 ounces shredded cheese (such as Mozzarella)

PREPARATION

01. Heat the olive oil in a pot over medium heat. Add the shallot and garlic, and sweat (2 to 3 minutes). Once the shallots are translucent and the garlic is fragrant, add the diced tomatoes. Bring to a boil briefly, then simmer, uncovered, for 5 minutes, stirring frequently. Season with vinegar, salt, pepper, and Italian seasoning, then remove from heat.

02. Divide the pizza dough into 2 equal portions and use a rolling pin to roll out on a lightly floured surface. Make 2 disks of dough as thin as possible, each with a diameter of about 9½ inches.

03. Preheat the oven to 400°F. Line 2 pizza pans (or a baking sheet) with parchment paper.

04. Set the pizza crusts on the pans, brush evenly with tomato sauce, and top as desired with peppers, mushrooms, tomatoes, olives, and chicken. Sprinkle generously with the cheese and bake for about 11 to 13 minutes, depending on how crispy you like your crust. Serve immediately.

GIBRALTAR'S

MAHI-MAHI

Little Mouse, Gibraltar's hometown on Solace, is in the middle of the desert, but there is a lot more going on beneath the surface. Like water! Confusing but true. There's a surprising amount of sea life under the waves of the Nostos Ocean, and the marine branch of S.A.R.A.S. (Search and Rescue Association of Solace) loves to catch what they can between emergency calls. According to Gibraltar, all that seafood has let his family and all the residents of Little Mouse keep the culinary traditions of their ancestors alive, including this tropical dish.

YIELD
4 SERVINGS

COOK TIME
20 MINS (plus 30 mins marinating time)

DIFFICULTY
SILVER

INGREDIENTS

Peel and fruit of ½ orange
Peel and fruit of ½ lime
Peel and fruit of ¼ grapefruit
Juice of ½ orange
1 teaspoon minced fresh ginger
1 tablespoon turbinado or raw sugar
1 tablespoon soy sauce
1 tablespoon rice wine vinegar
1 cucumber, roughly cubed
1 small red chili, minced
2 tablespoons olive oil, plus more for the fish
4 mahi-mahi filets, about 6 ounces each
Salt
Pepper
Cooked rice

PREPARATION

01. Combine orange, lime, and grapefruit peels with the orange juice, ginger, sugar, soy sauce, and the vinegar in a small pot. Bring to a boil over medium heat, stirring frequently. Simmer for about 5 to 8 minutes, until the sauce has thickened noticeably. Lower the heat to low, stir in the fruit of the orange, lime, and grapefruit, and allow to stand for several minutes so the flavors can meld.

02. Meanwhile, combine the cucumber, chili, and 2 tablespoons of oil in a large bowl.

03. Oil the fish fillets on all sides and season to taste with salt and pepper.

04. Heat a large frying pan over medium heat. Add the fish fillets and cook for 2 minutes on each side. Arrange on plates with the chili-cucumber salad and cooked rice, then drizzle with sauce to serve.

BLOODHOUND'S

BEHEMOTH BURGER

My friend Bloodhound is very different from my friend Mirage. While Mirage loves to chat while grilling—even when he gets distracted and burns things—Bloodhound is silent and focused. Hey, they're like that in the arena, too. I guess cooking and fighting aren't so different. Oh no, I hope I don't get fired from being a Legend! Either way, Mirage always says variety is the spice of life, so I'm glad to have such different friends. Oh, Bloodhound is looking at me. I don't know if they're annoyed or happy because of the mask, but their raven seems angry. That's normal, though. Maybe the burger will distract my not-quite-a-friend Artur before he tries to peck me again.

YIELD
1 BEHEMOTH BURGER
(serves 2 to 3)

COOK TIME
45 MINS
(including time for flavors to meld)

DIFFICULTY
GOLD

INGREDIENTS

1¼ pounds ground beef
1 egg
3 tablespoons teriyaki sauce
2 tablespoons onion powder
2 tablespoons garlic powder
1 tablespoon salt
Black pepper, freshly ground
1 tablespoon vegetable oil, plus more as needed
1 tablespoon turbinado or raw sugar
1 red onion, sliced into thin rings
1 teaspoon apple cider vinegar
16 strips bacon
1 large hamburger bun
Lettuce, to taste
8 slices Cheddar cheese
Pickles, drained, to taste
1 large tomato, sliced
BBQ sauce, to taste

Additional equipment
Long metal skewer (or Bloodhound's Heirloom Knife)

PREPARATION

01. In a bowl, combine the ground meat with the egg, teriyaki sauce, onion powder, garlic powder, salt, and pepper. Refrigerate for 15 minutes for the flavors to meld.

02. Meanwhile, heat the oil in a large pan over medium heat. Once the oil is hot, add the sugar and the onions and caramelize, stirring occasionally, for about 3 to 4 minutes. Once the sugar has melted and the onions are brown, deglaze with the vinegar and reduce for 2 minutes. Remove the onions from the pan and set aside.

03. Shape the refrigerated meat into 4 equal patties. Raise the heat to high, add more oil if necessary, and brown all 4 patties on both sides, about 3 minutes per side, turning only once. Season to taste with salt and pepper and set on paper towels on a plate to drain.

04. Add the bacon to the still-hot pan and fry on both sides until crisp. (If there is too much oil in the pan, use paper towels to soak up most of it first.) Set the cooked bacon on the same plate as the patties to drain.

Assemble the Behemoth Burger:

05. Cut open the hamburger bun, briefly toast the cut sides in a toaster, and top the lower half of the bun as follows: lettuce on the bottom, then a patty, then 2 strips of bacon, then 2 slices of cheese, followed by a heaping serving of pickles, caramelized onions, tomato slices, and BBQ sauce. Repeat with a second patty topped with cheese, bacon, lettuce, tomatoes, onions, and sauce. Repeat until the burger has 4 "levels," then finish with a heaping serving of lettuce and BBQ sauce. Place the top half of the bun on top, gently press into place, and carefully insert a long metal skewer (or Bloodhound's Heirloom Knife) through the entire burger to hold it together. Serve promptly. Excellent with Golden Chips (Page 104) or Steakhouse Fries (Page 84).

NESSIE'S

EASTER EGG SALAD PIZZA

I have seen so many amazing things since I woke up in a warehouse with no memories. I've watched behemoths step right over my head, grappled at high speed through the night skies of Malta, and visited alternate realities looking for a disassembled, disembodied head (of my best girlfriend!). I've seen lots of human emotions, including joy, sadness, and fear; I've felt them myself, too. And after all that, I learned the one thing I know for sure to be true: everybody loves pizza.

YIELD
2 PIZZAS

COOK TIME
45 MINS (plus 3 hours for flavors to meld)

DIFFICULTY
SILVER

INGREDIENTS

Egg Salad

8 eggs

2 tablespoons mayonnaise

Pinch of salt, plus more to taste

Pinch of pepper, plus more to taste

1 tablespoon vinegar

2 tablespoons sour cream

1 teaspoon Dijon mustard (or other moderately spicy mustard)

½ bunch fresh chives, minced

Pizza

1 tablespoon olive oil

1 shallot, minced

1 garlic clove, minced

8 ounces canned diced tomatoes

½ teaspoon balsamic vinegar

Salt

Pepper

2 tablespoons Italian seasoning

1 pound ready-made pizza dough

Flour, for dusting

4 ounces shredded cheese (such as Mozzarella)

PREPARATION

To make the egg salad:

01. Bring water to a boil in a medium pot, then add each egg using a slotted spoon or skimmer so they are not accidentally damaged. Cook for 10 minutes, until hard-boiled. Use the slotted spoon to remove the eggs from the water. Immediately run under cold water to cool, then shell and chop 7 of the eggs finely. Shell and slice the remaining egg.

02. In a medium bowl, thoroughly combine the mayonnaise with the salt, pepper, vinegar, sour cream, and mustard. Add the chopped eggs, cover loosely with plastic wrap, and refrigerate for 3 hours so the flavors can meld. Stir again, add the chives, and season to taste with salt and pepper. Refrigerate until used.

To make the pizza:

03. Heat the olive oil in a pot over medium heat. Add the shallot and garlic, and sweat (2 to 3 minutes). Once the shallots are translucent and the garlic is fragrant, add the tomatoes. Bring to a boil briefly, then simmer, uncovered, for 5 minutes, stirring frequently. Season with balsamic vinegar, salt, pepper, and the Italian seasoning, then remove from heat.

04. Divide the ready-made pizza dough into 2 equal portions and use a rolling pin to roll out on a lightly floured surface. Make 2 disks of dough as thin as possible, each with a diameter of about 9½ inches.

05. Preheat the oven to 400°F. Line 2 pizza pans (or a baking sheet) with parchment paper.

06. Set the pizzas on the pans, brush evenly with a very thin layer of tomato sauce, and spread a thick layer of egg salad on each. Garnish with sliced eggs, sprinkle generously with cheese, and bake for about 11 to 13 minutes, depending on how crispy you like your crust. Serve immediately.

ROASTED CARTHAGE SPIDERS

I've learned a lot from being friends with Loba, especially that looks can be deceiving. She is very fancy, but also scary, and sometimes she does both at once. One of those times was when we went on a special trip to Gaea to hunt Carthage spiders for this recipe—she says these spiders almost ate her once, so now she eats them back. Yep, scary! Since Carthage spiders can be hard to find (Loba says that's "a bonus"), I've made some substitutions so it's easier for you to make at home without any of your friends knowing the difference. Oh! Looks are deceiving again.

ARTIFICIAL ADVICE
If you have fresh spider...I mean crab...legs, those will work as well!

YIELD
4 SERVINGS

COOK TIME
20 MINS (plus 10+ hours thawing time)

DIFFICULTY
SILVER

INGREDIENTS

4 king crab legs (frozen)
2 sprigs thyme
1 sprig rosemary
2 cloves garlic, minced
4 tablespoons olive oil
Pomegranate seeds, for garnish
1 lemon, cut into wedges

Additional equipment
Grill or grilling pan

PREPARATION

01. Thaw the frozen crab legs in the refrigerator overnight.

02. Carefully rinse the crab legs and use kitchen scissors to carefully separate at the joints. Cut into the legs lengthwise on both sides, starting from the joints, and cut the meat inside in half lengthwise with a sharp knife.

03. Wash the thyme and rosemary and pat dry with paper towels. Pluck off the leaves or needles and mince. Mix the garlic, oil, and minced herbs in a small bowl.

04. Brush the crab meat with the oil mixture. Cook in a grilling pan set over medium heat, or about 8 to 10 minutes over indirect heat on a preheated grill, turning once. Brush again with the oil mixture while grilling.

05. Remove the crab legs from the grill, sprinkle with pomegranate seeds to taste, and garnish each serving with a lemon wedge.

PROWLERS ON A STICK

As a master of living off the land, Bloodhound gave me even more culinary advice during a trip to World's Edge. Hooray for Legends bonding time! This time, we hunted down a pack of Prowlers, which Bloodhound says are rich in protein and other nutrients that organic lifeforms need to survive. They cooked the skewered meats right over the open lava flows of Talos! It was very impressive, but don't worry if you're scared of lava. I have directions for preparing your Prowler in a regular kitchen, too.

ARTIFICIAL ADVICE

The amount of time it actually takes to cook the meat depends on the size of the pieces and how well-done you like your meat. For medium (pink), the meat should reach an internal temperature of 140°F, and for well-done it should reach 160°F.

YIELD
4 SKEWERS

COOK TIME
30 MINS (plus 2 to 12 hours to marinate)

DIFFICULTY
SILVER

INGREDIENTS

6 tablespoons sunflower or similar oil
1 teaspoon sesame oil
2 tablespoons soy sauce
2 teaspoons Worcestershire sauce
2 teaspoons lemon juice
1 teaspoon balsamic vinegar
2 tablespoons honey
1 teaspoon mustard
1 garlic clove, pressed
½ teaspoon black pepper
1¼ pounds beef (steak or rump)
3 bell peppers (red, yellow, green) or 12 colorful mini sweet peppers
3 red onions, peeled and quartered
12 mushrooms
Coarse sea salt

Additional equipment
4 long skewers

PREPARATION

01. Start by preparing the marinade. Add the sunflower oil, sesame oil, soy sauce, Worcestershire sauce, lemon juice, vinegar, honey, mustard, garlic, and pepper to a small bowl and stir gently to combine.

02. Place the beef on a cutting board and use a large, sharp knife to cut it into bite-size pieces. Cut the pieces the same size so they cook evenly.

03. Place the meat and marinade in a large freezer bag and seal the bag. Vigorously massage the marinade into the meat and refrigerate for at least 2 hours, ideally overnight.

04. Meanwhile, wash the bell peppers, cut them in half, remove the core, and cut them into bite-size pieces.

05. Place the meat, onions, mushrooms, and peppers alternately on the skewers. Sprinkle the skewers on all sides with coarse sea salt. Pour the rest of the marinade in a small bowl.

06. If you are using a grill to prepare this dish, grill the skewers on all sides for about 8 minutes over medium heat on a preheated grill. Alternatively, cook them for the same length of time in a large, flat pan over medium heat. While the skewers are cooking, brush them on all sides with the remaining marinade.

07. If you are using the oven to prepare the skewers, preheat to 425°F and line a baking sheet with parchment paper. Place the skewers on the paper and cook for about 12 to 15 minutes in the oven, turning once. Brush the top side of the skewers regularly with the remaining marinade.

08. Once the meat is cooked, either serve the skewers whole or remove the meat and vegetables and set on a large serving plate. Enjoy promptly.

FUSE'S

THREE KINDS OF FRIED SAUSAGE

Like many Legends, Fuse used to have a lot of fun doing things that are against the law, at least on the planets that have laws. He spent many nights surviving off the land, cooking meals with whatever he could find. Even when he became a fighter in the Bonecage, he would still end his nights frying sausage "the old-fashioned way" for his friends after a match. So, while we tried to make this recipe at the Paradise Lounge, Fuse insisted the right way to prepare these sausages was under a starry sky over a portable gas burner. Though it took a lot longer to cook everything, the beautiful view and time spent with a friend made it even more fun—and tastier!

YIELD
3 SERVINGS

COOK TIME
75 MINS

DIFFICULTY
SILVER

INGREDIENTS

Pepper Sauce

1 tablespoon vegetable oil
1 large onion
1 garlic clove, minced
1 tablespoon tomato paste
3 bell peppers (green, yellow, red), diced
10 ounces canned diced tomatoes
2 tablespoons balsamic vinegar
1 tablespoon Worcestershire sauce
1 teaspoon smoked paprika
½ teaspoon curry powder
Salt
Pepper

Continued on page 83

PREPARATION

To make the pepper sauce:

01. Heat the oil in a pot over medium heat. Once the oil is hot, add the onions and garlic and sauté on all sides for 2 to 3 minutes, until translucent. Add the tomato paste and cook together briefly. Add the bell peppers, stir well to combine, and cook for 5 minutes.
02. Add the canned tomatoes, vinegar, Worcestershire sauce, paprika, and curry powder, stir well to combine, and simmer, stirring occasionally for about 5 to 8 minutes, until the vegetables are tender. Season the sauce with salt, pepper, and, if desired, a pinch of chili powder. Keep warm until serving.

To make the onion sauce:

03. Melt the clarified butter in a nonstick pan over medium heat. Add the sugar and onions and caramelize for 2 to 3 minutes.
04. Add the pancetta and brown on all sides. Stir in the tomato paste and cook together briefly. Sprinkle evenly with flour and reduce for a few minutes, stirring frequently.
05. When hardly any liquid remains in the pan, deglaze with the malt beer and vegetable stock and briefly bring to a boil. Season with salt, pepper, and caraway and reduce, uncovered, for 5 to 6 minutes, until the onion sauce is thick. Keep warm until serving.

To make the curry sauce:

06. Combine the oil, ketchup, and beef stock in a small pot and bring to a boil over high heat, stirring frequently. Simmer for 1 minute. Add the curry powder, cayenne pepper, broth, sugar, salt, pepper, and vinegar, stir well to combine, and simmer, uncovered, for 3 minutes. Remove from heat and allow to cool briefly. Keep warm until serving.

FUSE'S

THREE KINDS OF FRIED SAUSAGE

Continued from page 81

Pinch of chili powder (optional)

Onion Sauce
1 tablespoon clarified butter (ghee)
Pinch of turbinado or raw sugar
4 large onions, sliced into rings
4 ounces pancetta
1 teaspoon tomato paste
2 tablespoons flour
5 ounces malt beer
½ cup vegetable stock
Salt
Pepper
Caraway

Curry Sauce
2 teaspoons olive oil
½ cup tomato ketchup
4 tablespoons beef stock
2 tablespoons curry powder, plus more for sprinkling
½ teaspoon cayenne pepper
½ teaspoon powdered vegetable stock
2 tablespoons sugar
½ teaspoon salt
Pinch of pepper
Dash of apple cider vinegar

Sausage
3 tablespoons sunflower oil, divided
3 pork bratwursts
3 beef bratwursts
3 chicken bratwursts

To assemble the dish:

07. Meanwhile, poke the bratwursts with a knife at about 1-inch intervals so they do not burst open when cooking in the pan.

08. Heat sunflower oil in a nonstick pan over medium heat. Working in batches of 3 bratwursts of the same type, cook the sausages, turning occasionally for about 5 to 7 minutes, until they are brown on all sides. Remove from the pan, set on a large plate, and keep warm in the preheated oven at 160°F until serving. Repeat these steps to cook all of the sausages.

09. Once all of the bratwursts are cooked, serve them whole or slice them into bite-size pieces on a cutting board and place each kind of sausage on a separate large plate. Generously cover the pork sausages with curry sauce and sprinkle with additional curry powder. Serve the beef sausages with the onion sauce, then the chicken bratwursts with the pepper sauce. Serve with Golden Chips (Page 104) or Steakhouse Fries (Page 84).

PEPPER SAUCE

REAL FINGER FOOD

Catalyst and I became friends right away because we have a lot in common—she uses liquid metal, and I'm made of metal! I spent some time with Catalyst this past weekend, and while she mostly stayed focused on her readings (sometimes with books and sometimes with cards, and sometimes even with subtitles), she did show me this quick-and-easy recipe for chicken fingers. She says they're easy to make, and even easier to eat, and they keep sauce and crumbs off her cards. Yum, eating fingers with fingers!

YIELD
4 SERVINGS

COOK TIME
75 MINS (plus at least 8 hours to marinate)

DIFFICULTY
SILVER

INGREDIENTS

Chicken Fingers

4 chicken breasts (about 7 ounces each)

1 quart buttermilk

1½ cups BBQ sauce

2¼ cups milk

2 eggs

4 cups bread crumbs

2 cups flour

9 to 10 cups corn flakes, finely crushed

1 teaspoon salt

1 teaspoon black pepper

Oil, for frying (depending on the size of your pot)

Steakhouse Fries

2 pounds potatoes (russet or similar variety)

5 teaspoons salt

1 teaspoon sugar

2 teaspoons smoked paprika

2 teaspoons hot paprika

1 teaspoon curry powder

½ teaspoon pepper

Oil, for frying (depending on the size of your pot)

PREPARATION

To make the chicken fingers:

01. Wash the chicken breasts, pat dry with paper towels, and cut into narrow, finger-length strips. Place in a large freezer bag.

02. In a bowl, combine the buttermilk and BBQ sauce, then pour the mixture over the chicken strips in the bag. Mix well so the meat is coated on all sides with marinade. Refrigerate for at least 8 hours and ideally overnight.

03. Once the meat has finished marinating, beat the milk and eggs together in a shallow bowl. In another bowl, combine the bread crumbs, flour, crushed corn flakes, salt, and pepper.

04. Heat the frying oil to 350°F in a large pot.

05. Remove the chicken from the buttermilk marinade and allow to drain briefly in a strainer. Dip the chicken strips individually in the milk mixture, then dredge in the flour mixture. Make sure the chicken is fully coated with breading on all sides. Set the breaded chicken on a plate.

06. Once the oil is hot, use a metal slotted spoon or skimmer to carefully place a few chicken fingers at a time in the pot and fry about 8 to 10 minutes, until cooked through and golden brown on all sides. Remove and set on paper towels on a plate to drain. To keep warm, cover loosely with aluminum foil until all the fingers are fried.

07. Serve with Steakhouse Fries, or Golden Chips (Page 104), and a small bowl of Firestarter Dip.

To make the steakhouse fries:

08. Peel the potatoes and slice into strips about ¾ to 1¼ inch wide. Place in ice-cold water for 10 minutes to extract the starch.

09. Meanwhile, combine the salt, sugar, smoked paprika, hot paprika, curry powder, and pepper in a small bowl.

10. Remove the fries from the ice water and pat dry thoroughly with paper towels.

Firestarter Dip

5 tablespoons salsa

3 tablespoons chili sauce

2 tablespoons steak sauce

¼ to ½ teaspoon sriracha sauce, to taste

Additional equipment

1-gallon freezer bag

11. Pour the frying oil into a deep pot and heat to 320°F. Add a potato piece to the oil to test whether it is hot enough; if the oil hisses and bubbles rise to the surface, the oil is ready. Working in several batches, add the potatoes to the pot (quantity depending on the pot size) and fry for about 4 to 5 minutes until they are pale yellow on all sides. Use a metal slotted spoon or skimmer to remove the fries, and place on paper towels on a plate to drain. Prefry all the fries, reheating the oil to the necessary temperature as needed.
12. Heat the oil to 375°F and fry the Steakhouse Fries in batches a second time until they are golden brown and crisp. Remove the fries from the oil and place on paper towels on a plate to drain.
13. Once all the fries have been fried and drained, place them in a large bowl and toss with the seasoning blend to taste. Serve promptly.

To make the firestarter dip:

14. Combine the salsa, chili sauce, steak sauce, and sriracha to taste (depending how hot you want your dip) in a small bowl. Mix thoroughly, cover with plastic wrap, and refrigerate until used. Stir again to combine before serving.

REVENANT'S

PROWLER DINNER

Simulacra are incapable of eating food. Revenant is a simulacrum. So, Revenant—

I know what I saw, Path! Okay, yes, it was from a distance, and the sun was in my eyes, and maaaybe I had a tiny bit of a concussion from Gibraltar's bom . . . bomba . . . rain of pain, but I know what I saw!

You believe Revenant was feasting on prowlers in the middle of the arena?

There were bones everywhere! And he'd torn them apart with his bare hands!

As a simulacrum, he has the strength to—

To feast on the flesh of his wildlife victims! His face was all covered in gore!

There are lots of things that can get you dirty in the arena. I need to power wash my grooves on a regular basis.

Well, when he gets a taste for the most dangerous game, don't come crying to me, tin can! Because he's probably going to eat me first.

YIELD
4 SERVINGS

COOK TIME
20 MINS (plus 45 mins resting time)

DIFFICULTY
BRONZE

INGREDIENTS

2-pound tomahawk (bone-in ribeye) steak

2 tablespoons sunflower oil

1 tablespoon buffalo milk butter (alternatively normal butter)

1 sprig rosemary

Sea salt

Freshly ground black pepper

Additional equipment

Large grilling pan

Meat thermometer

PREPARATION

01. Remove the meat from the refrigerator 45 minutes before preparing this dish and allow it to come to room temperature. Rub on all sides with the oil.

02. Preheat the oven to 285°F on the convection setting.

03. Grease a large, oven-safe grilling pan with the butter. Heat over high heat on the stove, add the rosemary, and brown the meat for 1½ to 2 minutes on each side. Brown the edges on all sides briefly as well, basting the steak with fat the entire time.

04. Once the meat is browned, loosely cover the pan with aluminum foil and cook the meat in the oven until done. Use a thermometer to keep track of the core temperature. For medium (pink inside), the temperature should be about 140°F to 150°F; for well-done, it should be about 155°F or above. (But no one wants that!) Continue basting the meat with the aromatic fat during this time as well.

05. Once the meat reaches the desired core temperature, remove it from the oven and allow it to rest for 5 to 10 minutes. Place on a cutting board and cut across the grain into 1-inch-wide slices, season to taste with salt and pepper, and serve immediately without any fancy garnish or fuss.

FR //02
ILITY COURSE
02

Don't know much about food from Boreas, but I'm always up for free food. You made sure this is *the* place to go?

I am very confident! Both Seer and Catalyst said that Okonkwo's is the best that Boreas has to offer.

Oh, wow, yeah, this place must be legit; those two never agree on anything.

FUSE'S

MEAT PIES

Our time together in the arena has taught me that there are few things Fuse loves more than explosions. Our time together outside the arena has taught me that one of those things might be meat. When I asked him what kind was in these pies, his answer was "Yes." Fuse says protein is what keeps you ready for a fight at a moment's notice, and this will put some hair on my chest. I don't know how a hairy chassis will improve my combat efficiency, but I'm excited to try it at least once.

I want to think you're going to do something fun like glue a bunch of hair to your chest, but you're just going to download some sort of fuzzball emoji, aren't you? Yep, there, uh . . . there it is. No no no, it's . . . it's very cute, good job.

YIELD
4 MEAT PIES

COOK TIME
2 HOURS
(including baking and resting time)

DIFFICULTY
SILVER

INGREDIENTS

Crust

1 cup butter, cut into cubes and chilled

1 teaspoon salt

½ cup plus 1 tablespoon buttermilk

4 cups plus 3 tablespoons flour, plus more for dusting

Filling

1 to 2 tablespoons olive oil, for frying

1 onion, diced

4 ounces pancetta

1½ pounds ground meat (mixed beef and pork)

Salt

Pepper

1 teaspoon freshly ground nutmeg

2 tablespoons Worcestershire sauce

3½ tablespoons butter, plus more for greasing

¼ cup flour

1 cup beef stock

1 egg

Additional equipment

4 pie pans (about 6 inches in diameter)

PREPARATION

01. Combine the butter, salt, and buttermilk in a small pot and bring to a brief boil over medium heat. Combine with the flour in a bowl and use a mixer with a kneading hook attachment to knead until a smooth dough forms. Cover with plastic wrap and refrigerate for 30 minutes.

02. While the dough is chilling, heat the oil in a large frying pan. Add the onions and sweat until translucent (2 to 3 minutes). Add the pancetta and sauté. Add the ground meat and brown on all sides, stirring occasionally. Season the meat with salt, pepper, nutmeg, and Worcestershire sauce.

03. Melt the butter in a small pot and stir in ¼ cup flour with a wire whisk. Add to the pan containing the meat, along with the beef stock, and simmer, uncovered, until almost all the liquid is gone. Remove from heat and allow to cool completely.

04. Preheat the oven to 320°F.

05. Use a rolling pin to roll out two-thirds of the chilled dough on a lightly floured surface until it is about ⅛ inch thick. Cut 4 circles out of the dough, each slightly larger than the pie pans (about 7 to 8 inches in diameter). Grease the pans and set a circle of dough inside each. Press the dough lightly at the edges and allow it to extend beyond the rim.

06. Knead the scraps together, roll them out, and cut out 4 round "lids" as large as the pans (about 6 inches in diameter).

07. Fill the crusts evenly with the meat filling, which should be as "dry" as possible, about ¾ full. Smooth the tops. Beat the egg and brush it on the rim of each pie. Set the "lids" on top so they fit tightly, press lightly to adhere, and fold the overlapping dough over the rims. Brush with beaten egg, cut an x into the top of each pie to allow steam to vent, and bake for about 1 hour or until golden brown. After the bake time, open the oven door, turn off the oven, and allow the meat pies to rest for 10 minutes before serving.

HOT MOI MOI

*Caustic invited me to dinner the other day! Sometimes he doesn't like me, but sometimes he does, so I was excited to spend time with him and see which it would be now. Also, because there was food there, I knew it would be great for the cookbook. He's very thoughtful. He asked me a lot of questions about how I'm doing, who I've been talking to, and if I've told anyone about Alexander Nox. Caustic and I talked about him before, when I said how interesting it would be if Tae Joon Park and Alexander Nox (who are both wanted fugitives) were related. It's fun to remember old times! Caustic also offered to share one of his favorite dishes by ordering it in front of me. For Caustic, that feels like a major olive branch!**

YIELD
4 SERVINGS

COOK TIME
45 MINS (plus 12 hours soaking time)

DIFFICULTY
SILVER

INGREDIENTS

6 cups dried black-eyed peas

2 tablespoons salt, for soaking, plus 2 teaspoons

2 small chilis, coarsely chopped

1 onion, coarsely chopped

1 tomato, quartered

2 hard-boiled eggs, roughly cubed

4 tablespoons dried shrimp

4 ounces canned sardines, drained

4 ounces canned precooked shrimp, finely chopped

1 tablespoon palm oil

2 tablespoons vegetable oil

Chili sauce

Additional equipment

2 food-safe sous vide or freezer bags

PREPARATION

01. Place the black-eyed peas in a bowl and add generously salted water to cover. Soak overnight (about 12 hours). Carefully rub the beans together in the water with your hands so the skins loosen, and remove the skins completely. Carefully drain the beans.

02. Combine the beans, chilis, onion, 2 teaspoons of salt, tomato, eggs, and dried shrimp in a stand mixer and blend into a fine paste. Remove to a separate bowl. Fold the sardines, precooked shrimp, palm oil, and vegetable oil into the paste and combine until the mixture takes on the consistency of very thick mashed potatoes. Divide the shrimp mixture evenly into 2 food-safe sous vide or freezer bags. Squeeze the excess air out of the bags and seal them securely.

03. Bring a large pot of water to a boil. Place the bags in the boiling water, cover, and simmer over medium heat for about 30 minutes or until the cakes are firm. Remove from the pot, remove from the bags, and allow to cool for several minutes.

04. Serve with chili sauce to taste. Enjoy hot or cold.

**There are no olives in this meal, that is just a common saying for becoming better friends.*

BANGALORE'S

SPICY BBQ PULLED PORK SLIDERS

When Bangalore said she would be "bringing the heat" to our lunch today, I expected her to show up with a weapon. Which she did! But she said it was unrelated. Instead, the "heat" was in her pulled pork, which had many of our friends begging for water when they were done.

Yeah, she brought two weapons. Those things hit like artillery strikes. Ow.

YIELD
24 SLIDERS

COOK TIME
1 HOUR (plus 6 to 15 hours marinating and slow-cooking time)

DIFFICULTY
SILVER

INGREDIENTS

Pulled Pork

4 pounds boneless pork shoulder
2 tablespoons fine salt
2 tablespoons freshly ground black pepper
1 tablespoon turbinado or raw sugar
2 teaspoons ground coriander
1 teaspoon ground cumin
2 teaspoons spicy paprika
2 teaspoons chili powder
1½ cups vegetable stock
1 tablespoon olive oil

Coleslaw

About 12 ounces red cabbage, shredded
3 ounces carrots, peeled and shredded
1 teaspoon salt, divided, plus more to taste
2 teaspoons sugar
4 tablespoons white wine vinegar
4 tablespoons vegetable oil or other neutral oil
2 teaspoons Dijon mustard
1 teaspoon honey

PREPARATION

To make the pulled pork:

01. Cut the meat into 10 pieces of about the same size. Combine the seasonings and stock in a bowl. Place the meat in a large freezer bag and add the seasoning mixture. Seal the bag, then briefly massage the seasoning into the meat. Refrigerate for at least 3 hours—ideally overnight—to marinate.

02. Preheat the oven to 320°F.

03. Heat the oil in a large, oven-safe pot over medium heat, then brown the marinated meat for about 2½ minutes on each side. As soon as the meat is browned, pour the marinade over it, cover the pot, and set in the oven. Slow-cook for 3 hours; starting at 1½ hours, check regularly to see whether there is still enough liquid in the pot. If not, add water so the meat is always covered with fluid. At the end of the cooking time, the liquid should cover only the bottom of the pot.

04. The meat is done when it pulls apart effortlessly with a fork. Transfer the meat to a bowl and allow to cool briefly. Use 2 forks to shred the meat, mixing the juices from the pan in with the meat. Now the pulled pork is ready to use.

05. While the pork is cooking, prepare the coleslaw and BBQ sauce.

To make the coleslaw:

06. Combine the shredded cabbage and carrots with ½ teaspoon of salt and the sugar in a bowl and knead vigorously by hand until the cabbage has softened noticeably.

07. Combine the vinegar, oil, mustard, and honey and the remaining ½ teaspoon of salt in a separate bowl. Pour over the cabbage and combine thoroughly. Cover loosely with plastic wrap and refrigerate for at least 30 minutes. Add more salt to taste if necessary.

08. Mix thoroughly again before use. Keep refrigerated.

BBQ Sauce

1 tablespoon vegetable oil or other neutral oil, for frying

½ medium onion, diced

1 garlic clove, minced

1 teaspoon smoked paprika

¾ teaspoon ground coriander

2 tablespoons tomato paste

3 tablespoons white wine or apple cider vinegar

13.5-ounce can tomato purée

2 to 3 tablespoons turbinado or raw sugar

1½ tablespoons Worcestershire sauce

1 tablespoon Dijon mustard

3 tablespoons orange juice

½ teaspoon fine salt

To serve

24 mini brioche slider buns

To make the BBQ sauce:

09. Heat the oil in a frying pan over medium heat. Add the onions and sauté for 3 to 5 minutes, until golden brown on all sides. Add the garlic and fry for 1 minute. Add the paprika, coriander, and tomato paste, stir well to combine, and cook for a few more minutes. Deglaze with the vinegar and immediately add the tomato purée, sugar, Worcestershire sauce, mustard, orange juice, and salt. Reduce, uncovered, for 10 minutes, until the sauce is about the consistency of ketchup.

10. The BBQ sauce can be used as is, including the onions. Alternatively, if you prefer a finer sauce, sieve it or purée to taste using an immersion blender. If the sauce becomes too thick, add water a small bit at a time until the sauce is the desired consistency. Keep refrigerated.

To assemble the sliders:

11. Cut the mini buns in half and toast the cut sides. Garnish the bottom halves of the buns as desired with pulled pork and coleslaw and drizzle generously with the BBQ sauce. Place the top halves of the buns on top and press lightly to adhere. Serve promptly, ideally together on a large platter for the ravenous horde to attack after battle!

"Life's never bleak with
Chickenbique"
Chickenbique

"Chickenbique is magnifique!" Hmm. Or maybe, "Chickenbique, where dining is peak!"

Path, what're you doing?

I was trying to come up with a catchy slogan for the Chickenbique section of the cookbook.

I, uh, I think you're good, bud. You're giving them a whole chapter, that's all the free advertising they need.

CINNABEAKS

The people who made Chickenbique really love chicken! They love it so much they made their cinnamon buns look like chicken beaks. It's confusing, because people don't usually eat the beak. That seems like a questionable business decision. I will have to ask Mirage about this—he's more familiar with questionable business decisions than anyone I know.

YIELD
16 CINNAMON BUNS

COOK TIME
45 MINS (plus at least 1 hour for dough to rise)

DIFFICULTY
GOLD

INGREDIENTS

2 cups milk

1 packet (2¼ teaspoons) active dry yeast

6 tablespoons sugar

6¼ cups flour, plus more as needed

1 tablespoon salt

1 teaspoon cinnamon

8½ tablespoons softened butter, room temperature

32 black poppy seeds, for decorating

PREPARATION

01. Warm the milk to lukewarm and combine it with the yeast and sugar in a small bowl. Cover with a clean dishcloth and allow to rest for 5 minutes at room temperature.

02. Add the flour, salt, cinnamon, and butter and knead about 6 to 8 minutes, until a soft, smooth dough forms. If the dough is not firm enough, add flour as needed. Allow to rise, covered, at room temperature for at least 1 hour or until the dough has significantly increased in volume.

03. Preheat the oven to 400°F on the convection setting. Line 2 baking sheets with parchment paper.

04. Knead the dough well again (about 2 to 3 minutes) and divide into 16 equal pieces. Roll out the pieces of dough to about 6 inches long and shape into a knot. Use your fingers to shape the top end piece into a bird's head with a pointy beak. Use a small, sharp knife to cut into the bottom ends a few times to form tails. Press a black poppy seed into each bird where an eye should be. Place the birds on the baking sheets, allowing space between them.

05. Bake for about 15 to 18 minutes, until golden brown. Remove from the pans and allow to cool for several minutes. These are best enjoyed while still warm.

BUCK BUCK BANG

Hmm, I've collated the data from my logs, and it says most meals are served on a plate or in a bowl. Why does this chicken come in a bucket?

Buddy, it's fried chicken. It comes in a bucket. That's just, like . . . that's the rule. Been that way since . . . Earth, probably.

That's still a lot of chicken for one person to eat on their own.

Got to have enough for all of my holograms, don't I?

Wow, did you upgrade your holograms to need food? Do they get hungry? Could you make it so I can eat food, too?

Path, no, that . . . it was a joke.

Oh, I see! Ha ha, jokes are fun!

If I didn't know better, I'd swear that was sarcasm. Anyway, any drumsticks left in there?

YIELD
4 SERVINGS

COOK TIME
45 MINS (plus at least 6 hours to marinate)

DIFFICULTY
SILVER

INGREDIENTS

2 pounds mixed chicken
4 tablespoons paprika, divided
3 tablespoons sea salt, divided
3 tablespoons black pepper, divided
3 tablespoons chili powder, divided
2 tablespoons garlic powder, divided
2 tablespoons onion powder, divided
1 tablespoon turbinado or raw sugar
1½ quarts buttermilk
2¼ cups milk
2 eggs
2 cups bread crumbs
2 cups flour
9 to 10 cups corn flakes, crushed
3 quarts peanut oil, for frying

PREPARATION

01. Wash the chicken and combine in a large bowl with 3 tablespoons paprika, 2 tablespoons salt, 2 tablespoons pepper, 2 tablespoons chili powder, 1 tablespoon garlic powder, 1 tablespoon onion powder, and the sugar. Vigorously massage the seasoning into the meat and spread evenly around the surface. Cover completely with the buttermilk and marinate in the refrigerator for at least 6 hours (ideally overnight).

02. Combine the milk and eggs in a bowl.

03. In a separate, shallow bowl, combine the bread crumbs, flour, corn flakes, and the remaining 1 tablespoon of each of the seasonings.

04. Remove the chicken from the marinade and immerse directly into the milk mixture, coating evenly. Dredge in the bread crumb mixture so the meat is thickly coated on all sides. Set the breaded chicken on a plate, repeating until all of the meat is breaded. Dispose of the marinade.

05. Heat the peanut oil in a large pot until it reaches 350°F.

06. Place a rack on a baking sheet and preheat the oven to 175°F.

07. Fry the chicken in batches (being careful not to overcrowd the pot), turning repeatedly to cook all sides, for about 10 to 12 minutes, until cooked through and golden brown. Set the fried chicken on the rack so it will keep warm until it is served and the excess oil can drain off. Excellent served with Steakhouse Fries (Page 84) or Golden Chips (Page 104).

FISH & SNACKS

Chickenbique continues to make me question everything I know about food. I just found out they sell other types of meat, which is confusing when "chicken" is in the name. Rampart said that some people do not like chicken, which makes sense, but those people still might want to come here to eat, which does not make sense. She pointed out that I can't eat at all, but I still go to restaurants with my friends. Sometimes, the point of going to a restaurant is not the food itself, but the people you are there with . . . even if you get the fish.

YIELD
4 SERVINGS

COOK TIME
60 MINS

DIFFICULTY
SILVER

INGREDIENTS

Fried Fish

4 fish fillets, about 6 ounces each (redfish, pollock, pangasius, or tilapia)

2 tablespoons lemon juice

Salt

Black pepper, freshly ground

4 tablespoons flour

2 eggs

¾ cup bread crumbs

3 tablespoons clarified butter (ghee)

4 lemon wedges, for garnish

Fresh parsley, for garnish

Tartar sauce (optional)

Potato Wedges

1¾ pounds firm, waxy potatoes

4 tablespoons oil

2 cloves garlic, minced

1½ teaspoons salt

1½ teaspoons pepper

1½ teaspoons paprika

PREPARATION

To make the fried fish:

01. If necessary, use tweezers to remove the bones from the fish fillets. Sprinkle with the lemon juice and season generously on both sides with salt and pepper.

02. Spread an even layer of flour on a plate. Crack open the eggs onto a second plate or shallow bowl and whisk with a fork until the whites and yolks are combined. Pour the bread crumbs onto a third plate.

03. Lay the fish fillets, 1 at a time, in the flour on each side and shake to remove excess flour. Dredge the fish through the eggs so it is covered on all sides, then dredge in the bread crumbs. Place the fillets next to each other on a large plate.

04. Melt the clarified butter in a large frying pan (or, even better, 2 pans) over medium heat. Carefully place the fillets in the pan(s) and fry for 4 minutes, then turn and fry for another 4 minutes. Place 1 fillet on each plate, garnish with a lemon wedge and fresh parsley, and serve with Potato Wedges and a dollop of tartar sauce as dip if desired.

To make the potato wedges:

05. Preheat the oven to 350°F on the convection setting. Line a baking sheet with parchment paper.

06. Wash the potatoes thoroughly, dry, and cut into quarters.

07. Combine oil, garlic, salt, pepper, and paprika in a large bowl. Add the potato wedges and combine thoroughly so the potatoes are coated with seasoning on all sides. Spread on the baking sheet so the wedges do not overlap, and bake for 40 to 50 minutes, until golden brown, turning occasionally.

GOLDEN CHIPS

My trip to Chickenbique has reminded me that language can shift and change, so you have to stay on your toes to make sure you know what you're getting. On some planets, "chips" are thin, crispy fried potatoes, while on others, they are hot potato slices fried into fries but still called chips! They are at least both potato dishes, but there are also chocolate chips to think about. I wonder if those would go well with these golden chips?

YIELD
2 SERVINGS

COOK TIME
40 MINS

DIFFICULTY
BRONZE

INGREDIENTS

5 to 6 large, firm, waxy potatoes
3 tablespoons olive oil
Pinch of salt
Pinch of pepper
1 teaspoon paprika
1 teaspoon turbinado or raw sugar
Pinch of chili powder
½ teaspoon garlic powder

PREPARATION

01. Preheat the oven to 350°F. Line a baking sheet with parchment paper.

02. Wash the potatoes thoroughly, pat dry with paper towels, and slice thinly to same size (about ⅛ to less than ¼ inch thick) so they cook evenly. Leave the peel on.

03. Combine the olive oil, salt, pepper, paprika, sugar, chili powder, and garlic powder in a bowl. Carefully mix the potato slices with the seasonings.

04. Spread the seasoned potato slices on the baking sheet so they do not touch and bake for 30 minutes, until golden brown.

05. Ideally, served fresh from the oven with a small bowl of Firestarter Dip (Page 85).

Now here's my sort of place! Perfect for kicking back and celebrating my latest win with a big plate of noodles.

Not just when you win. I've seen you here after even a devastating loss!

It's a figure of speech, Path. Don't take it so literal.

In fact, most of the time when you're here, it's after you lose. I love this place, because it's comforting to my best fri–

Wow, hey, that stall looks great! What's going on over here...

MEDKIT TAKEOUT

"For Legends with a more refined palate, this premium snack box can be taken into the field as well. Whether you're camping out in the abandoned labs of Kings Canyon or the close quarters of Olympus, this expertly crafted Medkit Takeout can provide the perfect pick-me-up as you take a quick breather." Boy, these Syndicate-approved press releases certainly make writing my commentary easier! I can't eat the dish myself, but the many colors are pretty to look at. That bit of commentary was entirely written by me, Pathfinder.

ARTIFICIAL ADVICE
For more fun flavors, substitute smoked tofu or shrimp for the chicken in this dish.

YIELD
2 SERVINGS

COOK TIME
25 MINS

DIFFICULTY
SILVER

INGREDIENTS

9 ounces lo mein noodles
1 tablespoon sesame oil
2 eggs
3 tablespoons soy sauce, plus more to season
2 tablespoons oyster sauce
1 teaspoon sugar
1 to 2 tablespoons water
2 tablespoons peanut oil
7 ounces chicken breast, cut into thin strips
2 garlic cloves, minced
1 large carrot, peeled and sliced into thin strips
4 ounces soybean sprouts, drained
1 green onion, cut into thin rings
Pinch of pepper

Additional equipment
Wok (optional)

PREPARATION

01. Bring a pot of water to a boil and cook the noodles according to the instructions on the package (generally about 5 minutes), then strain. Rinse the noodles briefly in cold water and allow to drain. Combine with the sesame oil.

02. Beat the eggs in a small bowl.

03. Combine soy sauce, oyster sauce, sugar, and water in a separate small bowl.

04. Heat peanut oil over high heat in a large, deep pan or wok. Sear the chicken for 2 to 3 minutes. Add the garlic and carrot and stir-fry for another 2 minutes. Add the noodles and stir to combine.

05. Lower the heat to medium and stir in the sauce. Stir the beaten eggs into the noodles and allow to rest for 1 to 2 minutes, until the eggs begin to set. Fold in the soybean sprouts and onion and season to taste with pepper and more soy sauce if desired. Serve promptly.

MOCHI

I wanted to write this cookbook as a gift to all my friends and fans out there, but it's also been a gift to myself. I've found there are even more ways to prepare and serve ice cream than I knew! Instead of scooped into a bowl or cone, you can also serve it wrapped in soft, sticky dough. It's like a cream-filled donut, but the cream is ice, and the dough is rice. The fact that it can rhyme like that makes this dish even more fun to prepare. Thanks, self! I love it. This recipe doesn't use ice cream, but is a more traditional approach to mochi and it's almost as much fun.

YIELD
ABOUT 12 MOCHI

COOK TIME
ABOUT 2 HOURS
(plus 12 hours for soaking)

DIFFICULTY
GOLD

INGREDIENTS

Red Bean Paste

7 ounces dry red beans (ideally adzuki beans)

¾ cup sugar

Pinch of salt

Mochi

12 teaspoons red bean paste

1⅛ cups glutinous (sweet white) rice flour

⅜ cup sugar

1 cup water

Cornstarch, for coating

Powdered sugar, to serve

PREPARATION

To make the red bean paste:

01. Place the beans in a bowl and add enough water to cover them completely. Soak overnight (12 hours).

02. Bring water to a boil in a small pot over medium heat. Add the beans and cook for 60 minutes, until soft. Drain, reserving a little under ½ cup of the bean water in the pot. Return the beans to the pot, lower the heat to low, add the salt, and gradually add the sugar, stirring constantly. The bean paste is ready when the mass in the pot comes together into a slightly shiny paste.

03. Allow to cool for several minutes. Purée finely using an immersion blender and refrigerate in an airtight sealed container until used.

To make the mochi:

04. Measure 12 teaspoons of the homemade red bean paste (see above) and use 1 teaspoon at a time to form small balls. Place the balls on a small plate and refrigerate until used.

05. Combine the rice flour, sugar, and water in a bowl to form a thin batter. Pour into a nonstick frying pan and heat over low heat, stirring constantly with a wooden spoon. Continue stirring as the dough firms up in a few minutes and until it takes on a firm, sticky, stiff consistency.

06. Remove the dough from the pan and set on a plate dusted with cornstarch. Work the dough quickly, while it is still warm. Divide the mass into 12 equal pieces. Dust your hands with cornstarch and shape each piece of dough into a flat, round disk with especially smooth edges.

07. Place a ball of bean paste in the center of each disk and fold the edges up on all sides to seal around the filling. Twist the edges together and shape the "package" into a ball between your palms.

08. Mochi are best enjoyed fresh. Alternatively, they will keep for several days refrigerated in an airtight sealed container. Dust with powdered sugar to serve.

LOBA'S

ROLLS

Loba invited me to meet her at a fancy sushi restaurant on Psamathe, which reminded me of Tenmei. I used to work there! It's also on Olympus, so now I fight there, too. Someone changed its name before Olympus was evacuated, though, so now it's called The Reverie. That's a nice name. Anyway, Loba said that it's important to include the fanciest possible recipes in the cookbook to give a taste of the finer things. I said I wanted to use affordable, easily accessible ingredients, but she shrugged me off. She said I'm not selling actual fancy ingredients, but "the fantasy of how the other half lives." I reminded her I'm actually selling a cookbook, which just made her laugh.

YIELD
24 PIECES OF SUSHI

COOK TIME
45 MINS

DIFFICULTY
PLATINUM

INGREDIENTS

1¼ cups sushi rice
2 tablespoons shichimi togarashi seasoning
2 tablespoons rice wine vinegar
2 nori sheets
6 ounces surimi sticks
¼ cucumber
2 tablespoons Japanese mayonnaise
1 teaspoon chili sauce (such as sriracha)
Pinch of chili powder
A few drops sesame oil
½ ripe avocado, peeled and sliced into thin sticks
White and black sesame seeds, for garnish
Soy sauce, for serving
Pickled ginger, for serving
Wasabi, for serving

Additional equipment
2 bamboo mats

PREPARATION

01. In a strainer, rinse the rice until the runoff no longer looks cloudy. Drain, add to a pot, and carefully bring to a boil over medium-high heat with 1 cup of water. Once the rice is boiling, lower the heat to medium, cover the pot with aluminum foil, then seal with the lid and cook for 10 minutes. Turn off the heat and leave the rice to stand, covered, for another 10 minutes.

02. Place the rice in a large bowl, then sprinkle with the shichimi togarashi seasoning and drizzle with the vinegar. Carefully fold it in with a moistened wooden spoon. Allow the rice to cool slightly.

03. Wrap 2 bamboo mats in plastic wrap. Cut the nori sheets in half lengthwise. Wash the cucumber and cut it in half lengthwise. Remove the core and seeds and cut the cucumber into matchstick-size pieces.

04. Combine the mayonnaise, chili sauce, chili powder, and sesame oil in a small bowl.

05. Set ½ of a nori sheet on a bamboo mat, rough side down. Using slightly moistened hands, spread ¼ of the sushi rice evenly over the sheet, leaving a margin of almost 1 inch at the top edge. Set the second bamboo mat on top. Invert so the rice is facing down, then remove the top mat.

06. Spread ¼ of the mayonnaise mixture over the nori sheet, arranging one peace of surimi and a few sticks of cucumber and avocado to each side. Use the bamboo mat to roll firmly, bit by bit, but prevent the plastic wrap from being rolled in with the ingredients. Once the roll is complete, press lighty, sprinkle with white and black sesame seeds and set aside. Follow the same steps to make 3 more rolls.

07. Place the rolls on a cutting board and use a large, sharp knife to cut each into 6 equal pieces. Serve promptly with soy sauce, ginger, and wasabi.

COPYCAT VEGGIE CURRY

Even the most dedicated scientific minds need to take a break to eat every now and then, though Crypto, Caustic, and Wattson all seem annoyed by that. I don't understand why. I would love to eat; it's why I'm putting together this cookbook! Nat has more than a few fond food memories, though, including this curry recipe, which is a copycat of one of her favorite takeout dishes. According to Nat, the result is magnifique!

ARTIFICIAL ADVICE

Be careful with the red curry paste; some kinds are hotter than others. Some people might find even just two tablespoons too hot. Taste in advance, and use half the amount if necessary.

YIELD
2 SERVINGS

COOK TIME
40 MINS

DIFFICULTY
SILVER

INGREDIENTS

1 cup rice (such as basmati)
1 teaspoon salt
14-ounce can coconut milk
2 tablespoons red curry paste
1 onion, diced
1 garlic clove, minced
1 carrot, peeled and cut into bite-size pieces
½ red bell pepper, sliced into thin strips
1 small zucchini, thinly sliced
1 small head of broccoli, broken into small florets
¼ cup frozen peas
Juice of ½ lime
1 to 2 tablespoons light soy sauce
Chopped cilantro, for garnish
Salted peanuts, chopped (optional)

Additional equipment
Wok (optional)

PREPARATION

01. Place the rice in a strainer and rinse in cold running water until the runoff no longer looks cloudy. Add rice, salt, and 1½ cups of water to a pot and bring to a boil over medium heat. Lower the heat to low, cover, and allow the rice to cook for about 12 to 15 minutes, until all the water has been absorbed. Do not stir!

02. While the rice is cooking, skim the coconut cream (the firm mass that forms at the top of the coconut milk inside the can) and add it to the wok, along with the red curry paste. (Alternatively, a standard frying pan will do the trick!) Combine, bring to a boil over medium heat, and simmer until small, oily bubbles form.

03. Add the onion and garlic to the wok and sweat for 5 minutes. Add the carrot, bell pepper, zucchini, and broccoli, stir well to combine, and sauté on all sides, stirring frequently. Pour in the rest of the coconut milk and briefly bring to a boil. Lower the heat to low and simmer for 5 minutes. Add the peas and simmer for 5 minutes more. Season to taste with lime juice and soy sauce and arrange on plates with the cooked rice. Garnish with cilantro and, if desired, sprinkle with chopped peanuts.

VALKYRIE'S

JETPACK-ROASTED YAKITORI

Valkyrie seems uncertain of her culinary skills sometimes, but I don't think she should worry. She knows how to make cooking even more fun than it already is! When we were preparing these meat skewers, she turned it into a game to see who could finish prepping their portion first. She didn't actually say it was a game, but the way she sped up and kept looking at my work made it clear we were in competition. Fun! Then, when I finished preparing first and started grilling, she used her jetpack to cook all of her skewers at once and take the lead. Congratulations on winning our friendly afternoon hang-out time, Valkyrie!

YIELD
10 SKEWERS

COOK TIME
30 MINS
(plus at least 2 hours to marinate)

DIFFICULTY
SILVER

INGREDIENTS

5 tablespoons mirin
3 tablespoons sake
5 tablespoons soy sauce
1 tablespoon red miso paste
5 tablespoons turbinado or raw sugar
3 garlic cloves
1 piece ginger root (about 1¼ inches)
1 teaspoon shichimi togarashi
1½ pounds chicken breast, cut into about ¾-inch cubes
2 teaspoons light sesame seeds
1 green onion, green part only, finely sliced into rings

Additional equipment

10 wooden skewers

PREPARATION

01. Combine the mirin, sake, soy sauce, miso paste, sugar, garlic cloves, ginger, and shichimi togarashi seasoning blend in a small bowl. Place in a large freezer bag with the chicken. Seal the bag and marinate in the refrigerator for at least 2 hours.

02. Soak the skewers in warm water for 15 to 20 minutes shortly before preparing them.

03. Divide the chicken evenly among the skewers. Pour the rest of the marinade in a small bowl.

04. If you are using a grill to prepare this dish, grill the skewers on all sides on the preheated grill for about 5 to 7 minutes, turning 2 or 3 times. Alternatively, cook them on medium-high for the same length of time in a large flat pan. While the skewers are cooking, brush repeatedly (every 2 minutes) on all sides with the remaining marinade.

05. If you are using the oven to prepare the skewers, preheat to 425°F and line a baking sheet with parchment paper. Set the skewers on the pan and cook for about 8 to 10 minutes, turning several times and brushing the top sides of the skewers with some of the remaining marinade each time.

06. Sprinkle the skewers with sesame seeds, garnish with the onion, and serve immediately.

And this is our final restaurant. What better way to end our tour than with all the sweet treats we can eat. And by we, I mean you, Mirage, the one with a stomach!

I like sugar as much as the next guy, bud, but all good things in moderation. I can't get too carried away, I need to keep my shape for the . . . Games . . . Man, those donuts look good.

CHIN CHIN

I've eaten all of my vegetables and now it is time for dessert! That's a metaphor, but I literally enjoyed the process. There are many visually appealing desserts here at Indidi's, and I have a whole list of recommendations to check out. I'm starting with this favorite of Catalyst's, which is just one of many ways people fry dough as a snack. The crunch it makes when I squeeze it between my fingers sure is fun.

Yep, it's a fun crunch in your mouth, too, buddy. Helping you with this has been a lot of "eating vegetables," if you know what I mean, people at home? So I'm glad my dessert isn't just met . . . meet . . . meta . . . fake.

YIELD
4 SERVINGS

COOK TIME
15 MINS

DIFFICULTY
SILVER

INGREDIENTS

4 cups flour, plus more for dusting
½ cup sugar
3 eggs
3½ tablespoons margarine
4 teaspoons ground nutmeg
1 teaspoon salt
Oil, for frying (depending on the size of your pan)

PREPARATION

01. Add the flour, sugar, eggs, margarine, nutmeg, and salt to a bowl and knead until as firm as possible, using your hands or an electric mixer with a kneading hook attachment.

02. Spread the dough on a lightly floured surface and roll out with a rolling pin about ½ inch thick. Cut into strips about 1 inch wide and 4 inches long.

03. Heat about 1 inch of oil in a large pan over medium heat and add the strips of dough in batches so they do not overlap. Fry on all sides in the hot oil about 5 minutes, until light brown. Remove and set on paper towels on a plate to drain. Allow to cool for a few minutes before enjoying.

PUFF-PUFFS

Wow, there are a lot of recipes for fried snacks! Mirage was right: people really, really, really love sugary dough. They even go back to old recipes and make new changes, just to have more they can try. Gibraltar just made a party-size order of Puff-Puffs to share with Catalyst, Crypto, Seer, and Newcastle. It was a great fried dough celebration with friends. Oh, it was a friend dough celebration!

Did . . . did you just make a pun? Wow, Path, I didn't know you had it in you. Wattson's got some competition. (Not me, though. King of comedy, here.)

YIELD
4 SERVINGS

COOK TIME
30 MINS (plus 1 to 2 hours for dough to rise)

DIFFICULTY
SILVER

INGREDIENTS

3 to 4 teaspoons active dry yeast

½ cup sugar

⅞ cup water, lukewarm

3⅔ cups flour

2 pinches of salt

1 to 2 tablespoons cocoa powder

3 quarts (96 fluid ounces) vegetable oil, for frying

Powdered sugar, for sprinkling

PREPARATION

01. Add the yeast and sugar to a small bowl, stir together with ⅞ cup of water, and allow to stand for 10 minutes. Add the flour and salt and gradually add lukewarm water, one tablespoon at a time, combining all ingredients, to make a pliable, smooth dough.

02. Place half of the dough in a separate bowl and combine with the cocoa powder. Set the bowls in a warm place to rise for at least 1 to 2 hours, until they have significantly increased in volume.

03. Shape small, bite-size balls of dough with your hands and set them on a plate.

04. Heat the vegetable oil in a large pot to about 350°F. The oil is hot enough when small bubbles form on the handle of a wooden spoon inserted into the pot. Add the balls of dough to the pot in batches—only a few at a time—and fry for about 4 to 5 minutes, until golden brown on all sides. Use a metal slotted spoon or skimmer to remove the puffs and place on paper towels on a plate to drain briefly. Dust quickly with powdered sugar and enjoy as soon as possible.

DONUTS

My friends all have different opinions on which portable snack is the best to bring into the arena. Newcastle says the donut is the perfect choice, no question. They're perfect for a quick bite while hunkered behind his Castle Wall or for giving an extra jolt to a teammate as he revives them on the move. It's important to only take cake donuts, though, because anything with glaze (like these donuts!) or filling can make a weapon slippery or sticky. That makes me think donuts might not be the perfect arena snack at all, but Newcastle said that learning to operate within limitations is what allows us to overcome life's hardest challenges. Plus, they're too delicious to leave behind.

YIELD
12 TO 15 DONUTS

COOK TIME
40 MINS (plus 90 mins for dough to rise)

DIFFICULTY
SILVER

INGREDIENTS

4 cups flour

1 packet (2¼ teaspoons) active dry yeast

¾ cup plus 1 tablespoon milk, lukewarm

⅜ cup sugar

1 teaspoon vanilla extract

6 tablespoons butter, softened

1 egg, room temperature

1 egg yolk

Pinch of salt

About 2 to 3 quarts (about 65 to 100 fluid ounces) oil, for frying (depending on the size of your pan)

1¼ cups dark chocolate

1¼ cups white chocolate

2 to 3 drops red food coloring

Colored sprinkles, for decoration

Chocolate shavings, for decoration

Additional equipment

Donut cutter (diameter about 3½ inches); alternatively, use a water glass and a shot glass

PREPARATION

01. Combine flour and yeast in a large bowl.

02. Add the milk, sugar, vanilla extract, butter, egg, egg yolk, and a generous pinch of salt. Knead all ingredients together for at least 10 minutes, until a soft, smooth dough forms. Cover the bowl with a clean dishcloth and leave to rise in a warm spot for about 1 hour, until the dough has doubled in size.

03. Use a rolling pin to roll out the dough about ½ inch thick on a lightly floured surface. Use a donut cutter or a similarly sized water glass to cut out circles of dough. (If you use a glass to cut out the dough, use a smaller shot glass to cut a hole in the middle of each circle of dough.)

04. Place the circles of dough about 1 inch apart on a piece of parchment paper. Cover with a clean dishcloth and allow to rest for 20 minutes.

05. While the dough is resting, heat the oil in a large pot until the oil reaches about 340°F. Working in batches of 2 to 3 donuts at a time, add the dough to the hot oil (making sure not to overcrowd the pot) and deep-fry for about 2 to 3 minutes on each side until golden brown. Use a metal slotted spoon or skimmer to carefully remove the donuts from the oil and place on paper towels on a plate to drain.

06. While the donuts are cooling, using 2 bowls, melt the dark and white chocolate in a double boiler (or by heating in short intervals in the microwave). Remove some of the melted white chocolate from the rest and combine with the food coloring in a small bowl. Hold each cooled donut horizontally and dip it halfway into the desired melted chocolate, allow to drip briefly, then flip over and place the unglazed side on a plate covered with paper towels.

07. Decorate the donuts as you like using the melted chocolates and other decorations while the glaze is still warm, moist, and sticky. Allow to dry briefly before serving.

KOKORO

Another fried dough treat! This one is inspired by a traditional Nigerian dish. I learned this has been a popular, easy-to-make snack for all of human existence, or close to it. I wonder what it is that makes fried dough in all its shapes and forms so appealing to people. Is there some ancient truth hidden inside?

Path, bud, you're overthinking this. Sugary dough just tastes really freakin' good. That isn't a secret.

YIELD
25 TO 30 PIECES

COOK TIME
40 MINS (including cooling time)

DIFFICULTY
SILVER

INGREDIENTS

1 cup water

1 cup cornmeal

1 cup flour

2 tablespoons sugar

Pinch of salt

1 quart (32 fluid ounces) vegetable oil, for frying

PREPARATION

01. Bring the water to a boil over medium heat in a small pot.

02. Combine the cornmeal, flour, sugar, and salt in a medium bowl. Slowly add half of the dry mixture to the pot of boiling water. Stir until there are no longer any clumps. Remove from heat and allow to cool completely.

03. Once the mixture has cooled, add the rest of the dry mixture and slowly combine. Place the dough in a clean bowl and knead with your hands until firm.

04. Pinch off a generous hunk of dough and use the palms of your hands to roll it out on the counter into a rope about 8 inches long. Repeat with the rest of the dough.

05. Pour the oil into a large frying pan and heat over medium heat. Once the oil is hot, add the sticks of dough in batches (being careful not to overcrowd the pan) and fry for about 5 minutes, until golden brown on all sides.

06. Set the kokoro on paper towels on a plate to drain. Best enjoyed with a cool drink.

GRAN ABUELA'S FLAN

So many of Vantage's meals on Págos were built around survival and what she could get her hands on. That meant dessert was a special treat that she cherished most of all. Her favorite was this flan recipe passed down through her family—she says it's the perfect remedy for the "harsh cold of a frigid winter night." I thought insulation and a fire would be much better remedies, but Vantage has spent more time surviving frozen wastelands than I have, so I trust her.

YIELD
6 SERVINGS

COOK TIME
60 MINS (including setting)

DIFFICULTY
SILVER

INGREDIENTS

1 cup sugar, divided

2 tablespoons sweetened condensed milk

1⅓ cups whole milk

1 tablespoon vanilla extract

4 eggs

Chocolate shavings, for garnish

Additional equipment

6 ramekins or small bowls

PREPARATION

01. Spread ½ cup of sugar evenly across the bottom of a nonstick frying pan and heat over medium heat until the sugar gradually begins to liquefy. Once all the sugar has caramelized, pour evenly into the ramekins and let stand.

02. To make the flan, add the condensed milk, whole milk, and vanilla extract to a pot and heat over medium heat until the mixture reaches a boil. Remove from heat.

03. Vigorously beat the remaining ½ cup of sugar and the eggs together in a bowl using a wire whisk.

04. Preheat the oven to 350°F. Bring about 1 quart of water to a boil in a pot or electric kettle.

05. Use the whisk to stir the milk at a constant speed while slowly adding the sugar-and-egg mixture. Combine carefully and pour through a sieve into a clean bowl. Divide evenly among the ramekins.

06. Place the ramekins in a large casserole dish (or the same frying pan after cleaning) and then carefully add boiling water to the large dish so the water comes ⅔ of the way up the sides of the ramekins. Place in the preheated oven and cook for 30 minutes to set. Remove from the oven and the water.

07. Use a sharp knife to loosen the edge of each flan from each ramekin and refrigerate until completely cooled before enjoying. Before serving, place each ramekin briefly (for about 15 seconds) in hot water again, then carefully turn out upside down onto a plate. This will allow the caramel to liquefy again and drizzle beautifully over the flan. Sprinkle with chocolate shavings to taste and enjoy immediately!

KULI KULI

Perhaps it's the size of fried treats that people find so appealing? You could carry dozens of this kuli kuli without breaking a sweat!

Ah, I mean, it's nice when you're in a hurry. And, you know, any snack is portable if you try hard enough. This one night a group showed up at the Lounge with an entire wedding cake! They were snacking away on the thing between drinks.

I wonder if this would be a fun dish for a wedding? It is certainly fun to think about!

You know, not a single one of 'em was dressed for a wedding . . . Where'd that cake come from?

YIELD
4 SERVINGS

COOK TIME
25 MINS

DIFFICULTY
SILVER

INGREDIENTS

1¾ cups unsalted shelled peanuts

Cayenne pepper

Salt

2 to 5 tablespoons water

Peanut oil, for frying (depending on the size of your pan)

Additional equipment
Mortar and pestle

PREPARATION

01. Toast the peanuts in a nonstick pan over medium heat, then chop very finely in a blender or food processor. Grind them more using a mortar and pestle if needed, so you have a fairly smooth paste.

02. Place the peanut paste in a clean dishcloth and wring it forcefully to extract as much oil as possible. Knead and wring out again. If that's too strenuous, shape the peanut paste into a long rope, wrap it in a dishcloth, place it on a board, and work it with a meat tenderizer or rolling pin. Whichever method you choose, the goal is the same: to get the oil out!

03. Place the peanut paste in a bowl, season to taste with cayenne pepper and salt, and add just enough water to make the mixture smooth and pliable so you can work with it like dough without it cracking.

04. Use a rolling pin to roll out the peanut paste on the counter to between ⅛ inch and ¼ inch thick. Use a small knife or pizza cutter to cut into even, bite-size rectangular pieces.

05. Heat peanut oil in a pan over medium heat (not too hot!) and fry the peanut wafers on both sides for about 3 to 4 minutes, until golden brown. Make sure not to overcrowd the pan, and take care not to allow the wafers to burn.

06. Set the wafers on paper towels on a plate to drain and allow to dry completely before consuming.

STRANGE ICE CREAM

Mirage says it's weird that I love ice cream so much despite never having tasted it, but I don't think it's weird at all, because everyone else loves ice cream, too! Even if I can't eat it, preparing it is fun. I bet working in an ice cream parlor would be almost as great as being a Legend. Maybe even greater! Ice cream and Kings Canyon both have Rocky Roads, but one is tastier. Maybe I'll open my own ice cream parlor one day and make a whole bunch of new brain-frozen friends.

Oo, with Legend-themed flavors? Wattson-melon, Cinnamon Short-Fuse, Seer-eal Surprise? I'm partial to the Mango Mirage myself.

YIELD
ABOUT 3 CUPS OF ICE CREAM

COOK TIME
30 MINS
(plus 4 to 5 hours for freezing)

DIFFICULTY
SILVER

ARTIFICIAL ADVICE
The ice cream will keep for about 2 weeks in the freezer.

INGREDIENTS

Pistachio Ice Cream

4 ounces shelled unsalted pistachios (roasted)

1⅓ cups milk

3 egg yolks

⅓ cup sugar

1 cup whipping cream

To serve

Ice cream cones

Cocktail cherries, drained

Chocolate shavings

Additional equipment

Sealable container suitable for use in the freezer and large enough to hold at least 3 cups of ice cream

Ice cream scoop

PREPARATION

To make the pistachio ice cream:

01. Set the container in the freezer and freeze for 2 hours.

02. Roughly chop the pistachios and slightly toast them in a dry pan over medium heat.

03. Bring the milk to a boil in a small pot over medium heat, then remove from heat. Add the chopped pistachios and allow to stand for 10 minutes. Use an immersion blender to purée the pistachios and milk very smoothly in the pot.

04. Working in a bowl over a hot-water bath, combine the egg yolks and sugar and beat for 2 to 3 minutes until creamy and whitish. Add the whipping cream and pistachio milk and stir over the water bath for another 2 minutes. Transfer the mixture to a clean bowl and chill in the refrigerator for at least 1 hour.

05. Stir the chilled mass again, then spread evenly in the prefrozen container and seal. Return the container to the freezer and stir the ice cream mass with a spoon every 30 minutes until it has fully firmed up. Keep in the freezer until ready to serve.

06. To serve, remove the ice cream from the freezer a few minutes beforehand. Using an ice cream scoop, place the ice cream in an ice cream cone, garnish with a cocktail cherry, and sprinkle with chocolate shavings. Serve immediately.

WATTSON'S

CRACKLING ORANGE PARFAIT

Though Wattson likes experimenting in the lab and the kitchen, she says that sometimes a simple treat can be the most rewarding. I think Wattson has her own idea of what "simple" means, because this dish can take a long time to make, but it does only have a few ingredients. I guess when you spend most of your time coming up with solutions to complex problems, mostly in a bloodsport arena, the meaning of words can change.

YIELD
4 SERVINGS

COOK TIME
ABOUT 45 MINS (plus 5+ hours for cooling)

DIFFICULTY
SILVER

INGREDIENTS

Parfait

1 orange

1 cup cream

4 egg yolks

3/8 cup sugar

About 4 teaspoons Grand Marnier liqueur

Orange Sauce

Scant 3 tablespoons butter

3/8 cup sugar

1 cup orange juice

1 orange, peeled and chopped into small pieces

Grand Marnier liqueur (optional)

Additional equipment

Julienne slicer

4 soufflé dishes or ramekins

PREPARATION

To make the parfait:

01. Wash the orange, carefully pat dry with paper towels, and use a julienne slicer to slice off even strips from the peel (about 1 inch thick).

02. Combine the cream and peel in a small pot over medium heat. Bring to a boil, then remove from heat and pour through a sieve or strainer into a bowl. Allow to cool for several minutes at room temperature.

03. Bring water to a boil in a pot large enough to place a metal bowl on top. In that metal bowl, beat the egg yolks and sugar on the lowest setting with a mixer with a wire whisk attachment. Place the bowl over (not in) the boiling water and reduce the heat to low.

04. Raise the mixer speed to medium. Working in several batches, gradually add the cooked orange cream and continue to blend for 5 minutes, carefully mixing to combine after each addition. Remove the metal bowl from above the hot water, stir in the liqueur, and mix again briefly to combine.

05. Cut 4 slices off the peeled orange to fit the bottom of the ramekins or soufflé dishes and lay the slices flat inside. Pour the orange cream mixture evenly into the dishes or ramekins and freeze for at least 5 hours. Meanwhile, prepare the orange sauce.

To make the orange sauce:

06. Heat the butter and sugar in a pan over medium heat. Melt the butter and wait until the sugar is caramelized. Once the sugar solidifies again, deglaze with the orange juice and add the orange pieces. Stirring frequently, reduce for about 15 to 20 minutes. Remove from heat and stir in 2 to 4 teaspoons of liqueur to taste, if desired, once the sauce has cooled a bit.

To assemble:

07. Remove the parfait from the freezer and allow to thaw for 5 minutes so it is easier to remove from the dishes. (You may need to carefully run a bread knife around the inside rim of the dishes.) Place a small plate on top of each parfait, keeping the parfait centered, then carefully turn upside down so the parfait is plated with the orange slice on top. Drizzle with the sauce and enjoy.

ASH'S

SMOOTHIE

Being alive is one of the greatest gifts I can think of, and I'm happy just to be here at all! But being human must be a very different experience, because every simulacrum I've met seems sad or angry all the time. Ash is not nearly as scary as Revenant, but she is not always happy or friendly—actually, she's almost always not. But when I asked her if she remembered any other recipes she might want to share, she was happy to show me this smoothie, I think. She said it was fun watching the fruit get blended into an unrecognizable slush and that it reminded her of crushing her opponents beneath her Titan's foot during the Frontier War. I promise, you will not need to crush anything but tasty fruit to make this smoothie.

Path, bud, that's . . . wow. Opposites attract, I guess.

YIELD
1 SMOOTHIE

COOK TIME
10 MINS

DIFFICULTY
BRONZE

INGREDIENTS

4 ounces fresh blueberries
2 ounces baby spinach
1 teaspoon psyllium seed
1 teaspoon chia seed
1 teaspoon flaxseed
4 ounces coconut milk
Potassium carbonate (potash), for garnish (optional)

PREPARATION

01. Wash the berries and spinach and carefully dry with paper towels.

02. Add the berries, spinach, psyllium seed, chia seed, flaxseed, and coconut milk to a blender and purée very smoothly.

03. Pour into a glass, sprinkle with a bit of potash if desired, and serve immediately.

BAKED GOODS

Path, we just did desserts, why are there more desserts? We're supposed to be done!

"Baked goods" does not necessarily mean desserts.

Path, I can see the list, it's all cake and cookies!

And all made with love by our fellow Legends!

NEWCASTLE'S

RED VELVET CAKE

Mirage says red velvet is just chocolate cake with food coloring, but I see lots of differences! The most important is that Newcastle likes it better. He says it has an extra hidden layer. With the right frosting and a dash of sweet justice, any dessert can be the red velvet the world needs. He got quiet after that, but everyone who tried it smiled and said "Mmm!," so I'm excited to include it in the book all the same.

YIELD
1 CAKE (about 8 servings)

COOK TIME
80 MINS (including baking time)

DIFFICULTY
PLATINUM

INGREDIENTS

Cake

½ cup butter, room temperature, plus more for greasing

⅔ cup vegetable oil

2 tablespoons vanilla extract

1⅜ cups sugar

3 eggs, room temperature

1 cup plus 2 tablespoons buttermilk, room temperature

2 teaspoons white wine vinegar

Red food coloring

2½ cups flour

⅓ cup unsweetened cocoa powder

2 teaspoons baking powder

1 teaspoon baking soda

¼ teaspoon salt

Cream Cheese Frosting

1⅛ cups butter, room temperature

1 cup sifted powdered sugar

14 ounces cream cheese, room temperature

To serve

Freeze-dried raspberries, roughly crushed into powder, for garnish

Additional equipment

3 cake pans (about 9 inches in diameter)

PREPARATION

To make the cake:

01. Combine the butter, oil, vanilla extract, and sugar in a bowl to form a creamy, light-colored mass. Add the eggs and combine thoroughly until the consistency is similar to that of pudding.

02. Preheat the oven to 350°F on the convection setting. Line the pans with parchment paper and grease lightly with butter.

03. In a separate bowl, combine the buttermilk and vinegar with sufficient food coloring to lend the batter your desired deep-red velvet color.

04. In another bowl, combine the flour, cocoa powder, baking powder, baking soda, and salt and sift over the butter-and-egg mixture. Combine, then add the buttermilk mixture. Stir briefly, just until the dry ingredients are moist and all ingredients are combined. Divide the batter evenly between the prepared pans. Smooth the tops and bake for about 35 to 40 minutes. Remove from the oven and allow to cool completely in the pans before removing to serve.

To make the cream cheese frosting:

05. While the cake layers are cooling, beat the butter and the powdered sugar in a bowl with an electric hand mixer until the mixture is lighter in color and fluffier than before. Add the cream cheese and beat thoroughly to combine.

To assemble the cake:

06. Place a layer of cake on a cake plate and spread it evenly with a layer of cream cheese frosting. Place the second layer neatly on top and frost. Use a spatula to generously coat the entire cake with frosting on all sides. Sprinkle the top with crushed freeze-dried raspberries as desired and allow to dry briefly before serving.

LIFELINE'S

MIRACULOUS LIFESAVERS

Ajay is one of the best support Legends in the Games because she repairs spirits with as much care and attention as she does bullet wounds and blunt force trauma. Sometimes she sneaks an extra ration of her famous lifesavers into her backpack so her teammates are happy and fed after she makes sure they don't die. Ajay said the recipe was her mother's specialty, but she also rolled her eyes. I think this was sarcasm, because I've heard her say her mother's actual specialties are death and war profiteering.

YIELD
40 COOKIES

COOK TIME
40 MINS (PLUS 1 HOUR FOR COOLING)

DIFFICULTY
SILVER

INGREDIENTS

1 cup butter, room temperature
1½ cups sugar
3 teaspoons lemon zest
2 teaspoons lemon juice
1 egg
3 cups plus 1 tablespoon flour
1 teaspoon baking powder
¼ teaspoon salt
¼ cup pearl sugar

PREPARATION

01. In a mixing bowl, combine the butter, sugar, and lemon zest and beat vigorously with a hand mixer for about 2 minutes. Add the lemon juice and egg and continue to beat until well combined. Gradually add the flour, baking powder, and salt, scraping down the sides with a spatula after each addition. Cover the bowl with plastic wrap and refrigerate for 60 minutes.

02. Preheat the oven to 350°F and line a baking sheet with parchment paper.

03. Place the pearl sugar in a small bowl.

04. Using your hands, shape the refrigerated dough into even, walnut-size balls and roll each thoroughly in the pearl sugar. Press into the sugar slightly to adhere, then arrange the cookies about 1 inch apart on the prepared baking sheet so they will not touch as they expand. Bake for about 11 to 13 minutes in the preheated oven, until the edges are light golden brown.

05. Take the baking sheet out of the oven and allow the cookies to rest on it for 5 minutes. Remove to a wire rack to cool completely.

06. Store in an airtight sealed container.

MAD MAGGIE'S

FAIRY BREAD LAMINGTONS

Metaphors are fun! Maggie said this dessert is her favorite from Salvo, and that it represents the spirit of her people. The white cake she starts with is how the Syndicate wants Salvo to be: boring and plain. But the spirit of the Salvonian people can't be denied, and so it's full of lively flavor and covered in hundreds of colors. I'm confused how the metaphor still works when she takes a bite out of her planet and its thousands of free spirits, but she says I'm just overthinking things.

YIELD
ABOUT 26 MINI CAKES

COOK TIME
40 MINS

DIFFICULTY
SILVER

INGREDIENTS

7 ounces marzipan paste
⅔ cup hot water
½ cup sugar, divided
5 egg yolks
Pinch of salt
Zest of 1 lemon
5 egg whites
⅞ cup flour
½ cup cornstarch
1 teaspoon baking powder
1¾ cups white chocolate
7 ounces multicolored sprinkles

PREPARATION

01. Preheat the oven to 410°F. Line a baking sheet with parchment paper.

02. Dissolve the marzipan in a bowl with hot water. Add ⅜ cup of the sugar along with the egg yolks (set aside the egg whites), salt, and lemon zest and blend thoroughly using a mixer with a whisk attachment or a stand mixer.

03. In a separate bowl, beat the remaining ⅛ cup of sugar and the egg whites with a hand mixer. Use a spatula to fold into the lemon-yolk mixture.

04. Sift the flour, cornstarch, and baking powder into a separate bowl and combine, then carefully fold into the lemon-yolk mixture with the spatula. Continue folding just until no flour is visible.

05. Set the dough on the prepared baking sheet and smooth it into a square shape with a smooth top. Set on the middle oven rack and bake for 10 minutes. Remove, turn over the sponge cake onto a clean dishcloth, and carefully remove the parchment paper. Allow to cool for several minutes. Line the baking sheet with parchment paper again.

06. Bring a small pot of water to a boil and place a metal bowl over but not in the boiling water. Add the white chocolate to the bowl and melt, stirring occasionally.

07. Using a large bread knife, cut the sponge cake in half down the middle. Trim the edges as needed. Pour 2 to 3 tablespoons of melted white chocolate onto one piece of sponge cake and swiftly spread into a thin layer. Place the second piece of sponge cake neatly on top of the first.

08. Cut the filled sponge cake into even, bite-size cubes. Dip each cube into the melted white chocolate on all sides (or spread the melted white chocolate on the sides) and then roll in the sprinkles in a small bowl so the cubes are coated with sprinkles on all sides. Set on the baking sheet and allow to dry for several minutes.

09. Store in an airtight sealed container.

LIFELINE'S

"PAS ME DAT SUGA" COOKIES

Even outside the arena, Ajay tries to live up to the name Lifeline. Sometimes she visits friends she's shot to make sure they're okay, even when they were the ones shooting at her first. When she does visit, she'll bring D.O.C. for a quick patch-up and a tin of her favorite sugar cookies. She brought me cookies once, and while I could not eat them, I was able to make a cookie with a bite taken out of it appear on my screen, and that was a lot of fun, too!

The cookies are nice, but some money to fix all the bullet holes in my outfit would be a lot nicer. I've got an image to project, and my tailor's not cheap!

YIELD
ABOUT 40 TO 50 COOKIES

COOK TIME
40 MINS (plus 1 hour for cooling)

DIFFICULTY
SILVER

INGREDIENTS

3½ cups all-purpose flour
1 tablespoon baking soda
1 teaspoon salt
2 sticks (1 cup) butter
1 cup sugar
1 cup light brown sugar
1 teaspoon vanilla extract
2 large eggs
2 cups chocolate chips

PREPARATION

01. Preheat the oven to 375°F and line a baking sheet with parchment paper.

02. In a mixing bowl (or helmet), combine flour, baking soda, and salt.

03. In another bowl, cream the butter, sugar, light brown sugar, and vanilla extract with a fork.

04. Add eggs one at a time, mixing after each.

05. Gradually beat in flour mixture until it's uniform.

06. Add chocolate chips.

07. Form small balls of dough, approximately 1½ inches in diameter, and place on the prepared baking sheet.

08. Bake for 9 to 11 minutes, until golden brown.

09. Store in an airtight container.

STRAWBERRY COOKIES FOR NEWTON

Did you know that food is linked to memory? Horizon says that the smell and taste of different meals can stimulate parts of the brain that connect to old memories. Wow, humans are very complex. Horizon used to make these cookies for her son, so she says eating them again is the closest she's come to figuring out time travel, but I think she meant metaphorically. I hope she figures out time travel literally one day, so she can make those cookies for him again. That would be a happy ending, which I want for all my friends!

YIELD
18 COOKIES

COOK TIME
40 MINS

DIFFICULTY
SILVER

INGREDIENTS

1⅛ cups butter, room temperature
¾ cup sugar
¼ cup turbinado or raw sugar
2 eggs
2⅓ cups flour
2 ounces freeze-dried strawberry powder
1 teaspoon baking soda
½ teaspoon salt
⅔ cup white chocolate chunks
1¼ cups white chocolate chips

PREPARATION

01. Preheat the oven to 375°F on the convection setting. Line 2 baking sheets with parchment paper.

02. In a bowl, beat the butter, sugar, and turbinado sugar with an electric hand mixer for 3 minutes, until creamy. Add the eggs and continue beating for 3 minutes, until fluffy.

03. Combine the flour, strawberry powder, baking soda, and salt in a separate bowl, then add to the butter mixture. Combine with a spoon until the ingredients just come together. Do not overmix; the dough is perfect when barely any flour still shows. Fold in the white chocolate chunks.

04. Scoop the dough by heaping teaspoons and place about 1 inch apart in 3 rows on each baking sheet, for 9 cookies per sheet. Place the chocolate chips on top and press lightly to adhere. Make the cookies the same size so they will bake evenly. The dough will spread during cooking, forming perfect circles.

05. Bake each sheet of cookies for about 10 to 12 minutes, then remove. The cookies will still be extremely soft when removed from the oven but will firm up as they cool. Allow to cool on the baking sheets for 20 minutes. The cookies will sink somewhat and form a softer core.

06. Store in an airtight sealed container.

ROBOTS
Brewing Co.

Let me tell you, after all that work on the cookbook, it's nice to kick back with a drink and relax.

That is an excellent idea! A section for drinks would be the perfect way to wash down all the meals we've made.

So . . . we're not done?

Would it help if the drink menu served as advertisement for the Paradise Lounge?

Come on, bud, I'm tired, and . . . Wait, are we talking *free* advertising? Path, just when I think I'm out, you grapple me back in.

WRAITH'S

APPLETINI

I know exactly what you're thinking. You look at a woman like Wraith, with the black leather, the ghostly complexion, and the tragic backstory, you imagine she's going to be throwing back shots and brooding in a corner booth. And you'd imagine wrong. Turns out, Wraith loves a drink that tastes like a melted lollipop. She has those voices that keep her alive in a fight—maybe they're telling her an appletini's the secret to a long healthy life. Heck, maybe she just really likes the fake apple flavoring, I don't know. I don't question it. Last thing I need is her gunning for me for digging too deep. Like, literally gunning.

YIELD
1 APPLETINI

COOK TIME
3 MINS (plus 15 mins for cooling)

DIFFICULTY
BRONZE

INGREDIENTS

4 tablespoons vodka

2 tablespoons apple schnapps

2 tablespoons Cointreau liqueur

2 tablespoons apple juice

Handful of ice cubes

1 apple slice, for decoration

Additional equipment

Martini glass

Cocktail shaker

PREPARATION

01. Chill a martini glass in the freezer for 15 minutes.

02. Add the vodka, schnapps, liqueur, and juice to a cocktail shaker.

03. Add some ice cubes, close the shaker securely, and shake vigorously for 15 seconds.

04. Strain into the chilled martini glass, garnish with an apple slice, and serve immediately.

KOALA KOLA

Koala Kola is a specialty of Salvo, but it's getting more popular everywhere! Salvo is still a new member of the Syndicate Alliance of Free Worlds, meaning many planets have a hard time getting this tasty drink. Fortunately, my friend Fuse won the secret recipe in a Bonecage match! He said he got it from a Koala Kola factory employee who "had plenty o' bark, but no teeth to back it up." A lack of teeth would make eating solid foods difficult, so I understand why this man was so familiar with liquids.

Wait, why am I importing so much of this stuff if he knows how to make it himself?!

YIELD
ABOUT 16 FLUID OUNCES OF SYRUP

COOK TIME
75 MINS (including cooling time)

DIFFICULTY
SILVER

INGREDIENTS

2 oranges
1 large lemon
1 large lime
1 pod star anise
⅛ teaspoon ground cinnamon
⅛ teaspoon ground nutmeg
½ teaspoon dried lavender
2 teaspoons fresh ginger root, grated
1 small piece vanilla bean (about 1½ inches), cut in half lengthwise
2 cups water
1⅛ cups sugar
1½ tablespoons turbinado or raw sugar
¾ teaspoon caramel food coloring
Chilled sparkling water, for serving

Additional equipment

Glass bottle with cap (large enough to hold about 16 fluid ounces)

PREPARATION

01. Rinse the oranges, lemon, and lime in hot running water. Pat dry with paper towels and carefully zest using a small zester or grater.

02. Cut the tip off the anise pod and crush coarsely; save the rest of the pod for another use.

03. Combine the orange, lemon, and lime zest with the star anise tip, cinnamon, nutmeg, lavender, ginger, vanilla, and water in a pot and bring to a boil over medium heat, stirring frequently. Lower the heat to low and allow to simmer gently for 20 minutes.

04. Line a strainer with cheesecloth or paper towels and sieve the liquid through it into a clean pot. Squeeze the cloth vigorously to extract all the liquid.

05. Add the sugars and caramel food coloring to the pot and heat over low heat, stirring constantly, until the sugar has dissolved. Remove from the heat, allow to cool completely, and pour into a glass bottle with a cap that has been rinsed inside with hot water. The cola syrup will keep this way in the refrigerator for several weeks.

06. To make a glass of Koala Kola, pour 3 to 4 tablespoons of syrup into a glass and add ice. Add chilled sparkling water. Stir briefly and enjoy immediately!

TENMEI SAKE COCKTAIL

After our meal on Psamathe, Loba ordered a drink and went to look out the window at the city. It was very beautiful, but Loba looked sad instead of impressed. She said this place reminded her of Tenmei. I asked her why she would come somewhere to drink if it made her so sad, and she said sometimes where you want to be and where you need to be are two very different places. She needed to make sure she never forgot what Revenant did to her family. Then she finished the rest of her drink and said, "Maybe that's not the only thing I need to remember." I don't know what that means, but I hope dinner with a friend made her feel better.

YIELD
1 COCKTAIL

COOK TIME
3 MINS (plus 15 mins for cooling)

DIFFICULTY
BRONZE

INGREDIENTS

4 tablespoons sake

1 tablespoon sparkling dry white wine

1 tablespoon lemon juice

2 tablespoons cranberry juice

Handful of ice cubes

1 small lime wedge, for garnish

Additional equipment

Cocktail glass

Cocktail shaker

PREPARATION

01. Chill a cocktail glass in the freezer for 15 minutes.
02. Add the sake, sparkling wine, lemon juice, and cranberry juice to a cocktail shaker.
03. Add some ice cubes, close the shaker securely, and shake vigorously for 15 seconds.
04. Strain into the chilled cocktail glass, garnish with the lime wedge, and serve immediately.

OCTANE'S

STIM-ULATING MINT MILKSHAKE

Octane has been very kind to help me with recipes for the cookbook, which is good, because he works a lot faster than me. He chopped mint so fast I couldn't see the knife, used his bare hands to measure out ice cream, and said that putting a lid on the blender was "really more of a suggestion, amigo!" Mirage has also been very kind about helping with the cookbook, so I'm sure he'll be okay with the mess we've made, especially after he tries the result!

YIELD
2 MILKSHAKES

COOK TIME
10 MINS

DIFFICULTY
BRONZE

INGREDIENTS

⅞ cup cream
1½ tablespoons sugar
½ cup milk
2¼ cups vanilla ice cream
4 to 5 drops mint oil
1 to 2 drops turquoise food coloring
4 tablespoons chocolate shavings, plus more for garnish
2 dark chocolate mint cookies
2 leaves of fresh mint, for garnish

PREPARATION

01. Combine the cream and sugar in a mixing cup and beat with an electric mixer until stiff.

02. Add the milk, ice cream, mint oil, and food coloring to a stand mixer and purée. Add the chocolate shavings and blend again.

03. Divide equally between 2 tall glasses, topping each with a dollop of whipped cream and sprinkling with chocolate shavings to taste. Decorate each with a mint cookie and serve garnished with a fresh mint leaf.

SHIELD CELL SOFT DRINK

When the Syndicate heard about my cookbook, they decided to pitch in and provide a recipe as well; thanks, corporate friends! When the bullets are flying, nothing gets you back into the fray faster than a shield cell, and now you, too, can experience the electrifying jolt of a recharge with this refreshing soft drink. Collector's Edition mugs in both cell and battery sizes can be found at participating Outlands retailers.*

Be careful if you take any of those mugs into the arena with you, by the way. You accidentally try drinking a real shield cell, your tongue's going to be numb for at least a week.

YIELD
ABOUT 48 FLUID OUNCES OF SODA

COOK TIME
15 MINS (plus 3 hours for cooling)

DIFFICULTY
BRONZE

INGREDIENTS

9 lemons
5 limes
1 cup sugar
5 sprigs lemon balm, leaves only
1 quart ice-cold sparkling water
Handful of ice cubes

Additional equipment

Pitcher large enough to hold 48 fluid ounces

PREPARATION

01. Rinse the lemons and limes in hot water and pat dry with paper towels.

02. Slice 2 lemons and 2 limes into slices about ½ inch thick.

03. Squeeze the remaining 7 lemons and 3 limes and add the juice to a mixing cup. Add the sugar and stir gently to combine with the juice. Add the lemon and lime slices, cover the cup loosely with plastic wrap, and refrigerate for 3 hours so the flavors can meld.

04. To serve, pour into a large pitcher, add the lemon balm leaves to taste, and fill with sparkling water and ice. Stir briefly and enjoy promptly—an awesome way to quench your thirst in the heat of battle!

**Claims of friendship are made entirely on the part of the Legend and are in no way legally binding or indicative of an auxiliary relationship with either the Syndicate or Hammond Robotics.*

– Jacob Young, Director of Public Relations

OCTANE'S
COLD ONE

Octane says he used to love ordering this cocktail on trips to Olympus, especially since it made a mess and annoyed the other patrons. Because we already made a mess of the Paradise Lounge, it made sense to have Octane make this drink, too! Then Mirage came back and started yelling, and Octane laughed before sprinting out the door. Now Mirage has given me a mop. I do not think I get Octane's sense of humor.

You aren't leaving 'til you swab every inch! Is that . . . is that ice cream on the ceiling?! And why is everything so sticky?! Well . . . stickier than usual, anyway.

YIELD
1 DRINK

COOK TIME
3 MINS (plus 15 mins for cooling)

DIFFICULTY
BRONZE

INGREDIENTS

4 tablespoons Irish whiskey

1 tablespoon vanilla syrup

Handful of ice cubes

1 cup root beer

Additional equipment

Highball glass

Cocktail shaker

PREPARATION

01. Chill a highball glass in the freezer for 15 minutes.

02. Add the whiskey and syrup to a cocktail shaker, close the shaker securely, and shake vigorously for 15 seconds.

03. Add ice cubes to the chilled glass, pour the contents of the shaker over the ice, and fill with root beer. Serve immediately.

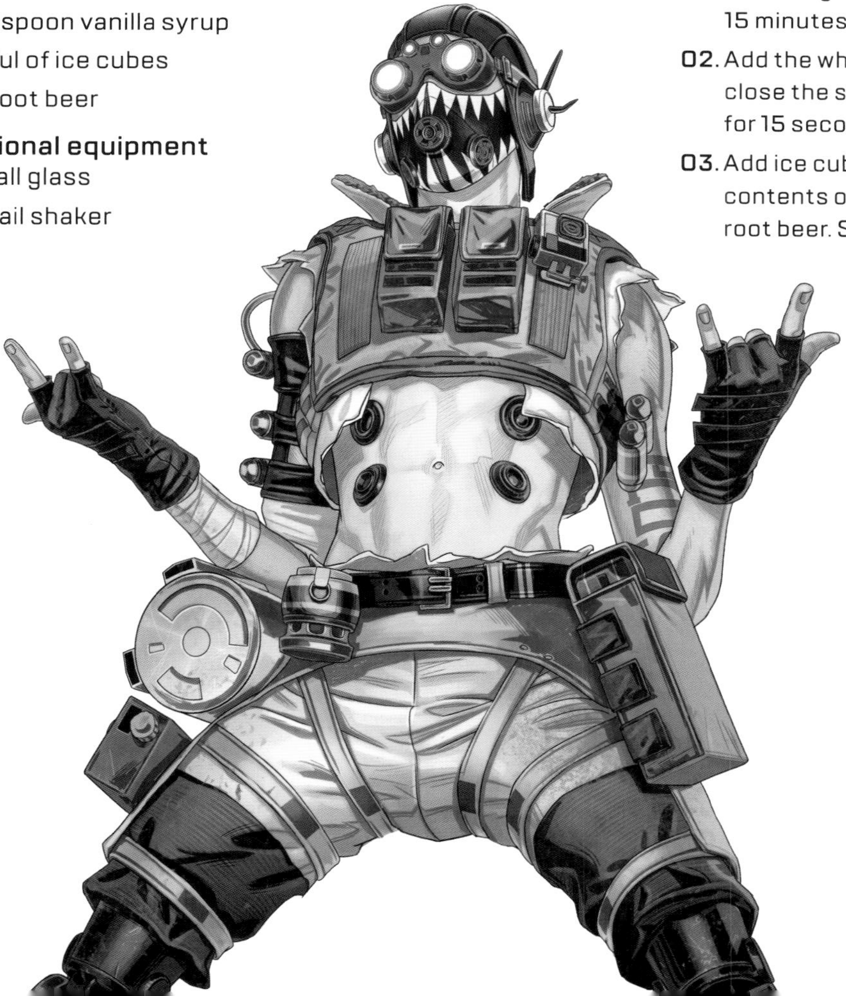

THE RAMPART

It's typical, you know? I put in all the effort to plan a party—decorate, come up with new drinks, print invitations—and it's 50/50 if anyone shows up. But I go out of town for a few days, suddenly everyone thinks it's a great time to hang out at the Paradise Lounge! For a while I wondered if they were getting through a literal hole in the wall, but now I think I've solved the mystery. I guess compared to starting an underground weapon trade out of my bathroom, breaking in to mix up a few drinks is pretty low-effort for Rampart. And at least she made one for me. It's tasty, but don't take that as an official endorsement; I doubt Ramya could afford me.

YIELD
1 DRINK (with enough leftover bubblegum rum for 4 more)

COOK TIME
10 MINS (plus at least 12 hours for flavors to meld)

DIFFICULTY
SILVER

INGREDIENTS

10 pieces pink bubblegum

10 ounces plus 4 tablespoons white rum

2 to 3 drops pink food coloring (optional)

Pink decorating sugar

2 tablespoons lime juice

Handful of crushed ice

4 ounces coconut milk

Bubblegum lollipop, for garnish

Additional equipment

Small bottle with cap (large enough to hold 10 fluid ounces)

Cocktail glass

PREPARATION

01. Clean and rinse the bottle, then roughly chop the gum so that the pieces are small enough to fit inside the bottle. Insert the gum into the bottle. Pour 10 ounces of rum over the gum. Seal the bottle, shake vigorously, and allow to stand overnight (at least 12 hours) so the flavors can meld. If more pink color is desired, stir in 2 or 3 drops of pink food coloring.

02. Spread decorating sugar on a plate.

03. Coat the rim of a cocktail glass with lime juice, then turn the glass over and dip in the sugar so that the sugar clings to the rim. Allow to dry briefly.

04. Place a handful of crushed ice in a stand mixer and add 4 tablespoons of bubblegum rum and 4 tablespoons of coconut milk, then blend thoroughly until no visible pieces of ice remain. Carefully pour ⅓ of the mixture into the glass.

05. Rinse the mixer. Add a handful of crushed ice. Add 4 tablespoons of uncolored rum and the remaining 4 tablespoons of coconut milk and blend until no visible pieces of ice remain. Carefully pour ⅓ of the mixture into the glass.

06. Alternate in 2 batches, adding the remaining pink rum and coconut milk and uncolored rum and coconut milk to the glass until the glass is full and has a lovely crown. Insert a bubblegum lollipop so the stick disappears into the cocktail. Serve immediately.

07. Save the rest of the bubblegum rum for later. It has a virtually unlimited shelf life.

HORIZON'S

FAVORITE TEA

Though she is separated from her son by the distance of space and time, I can tell Horizon still feels like a mom. When she saw how hard I was working on this cookbook on top of my time spent in the Games, she said I had to come over for a cup of tea. Even though I couldn't drink any, she said we should still sit and enjoy teatime. Horizon wanted to make sure I was taking some time for myself, and I was happy I got to spend it with her. I can tell she was a great mom, and also still is! Thanks to her, I've learned that holding a hot cup of tea and contemplating existence go very well together. Pinkies out!

YIELD
4 TO 5 POTS OF TEA

COOK TIME
15 MINS (plus 3 hours drying time)

DIFFICULTY
BRONZE

ARTIFICIAL ADVICE
This dry tea blend will keep for several months in a small sealed can or jar.

INGREDIENTS

Bunch of fresh mint

Sprig of lemon verbena

Sprig of fresh oregano (flowers and leaves)

Handful of fresh mixed edible flowers (such as elderflower, mallow, marigold)

1 tablespoon grated licorice root

1 vanilla bean, finely chopped

4 ounces black tea

Honey (optional)

Additional equipment

Mortar and pestle

Tea ball, or reusable tea bag with closure

PREPARATION

01. Preheat the oven to 140°F on the convection setting.

02. Line a baking sheet with parchment paper. Spread the mint, lemon verbena, oregano, and mixed flowers on the baking sheet and dry for 3 hours in the oven. Crack the oven door open with the handle of a wooden spoon so the steam generated inside can escape. Carefully pick the leaves and petals off the paper and dispose of the rest.

03. Using a mortar and pestle, roughly grind the dried herbs.

04. In a small bowl, combine the licorice and vanilla bean with the black tea. Add the ground herbs and stir to combine.

05. To prepare the tea, place 4 to 5 teaspoons in a tea ball and suspend inside a teapot. Pour hot (not boiling!) water over the mixture and steep for 4 to 6 minutes, depending on how strong you like your tea. Remove the tea ball and pour the tea into the cups through a fine sieve so no residue enters the cups.

06. Sweeten with honey to taste.

TEQUILA SUNRISE SHOT

Though everybody else gave me special drink recipes, Valkyrie said it's best to keep it simple, because the point of drinking is the drinking, and anything else just gets in the way. I thought making drinks with friends was super fun, but the clean-up after wasn't, especially when my friends would run away without helping. Valkyrie hasn't run off yet, and I've poured lots of shots, so this might be the most fun way to drink after all. She still won't let me try her jetpack, though.

Path, you've been keeping track of how many you've poured her, right? Valk, how many have you had? Valkyrie? Valkyrie!

Oh no, now Valkyrie has run off. Is fleeing the scene a normal part of drinking with friends that nobody has told me about?

YIELD
3 SHOTS

COOK TIME
5 MINS

DIFFICULTY
SILVER

INGREDIENTS

3 tablespoons tequila

5 tablespoons orange juice

Grenadine

Additional equipment
3 tall shot glasses

PREPARATION

01. Pour 1 tablespoon of tequila into each glass.

02. Pour 5 teaspoons of orange juice into each glass. The glasses will be ¾ full.

03. Carefully pour the grenadine over the back of a spoon into each glass, using as much or as little as desired. The difference in density between the liquids will create different-colored layers. Is it magic? No! It's science.

WITT'S WHISKEY

All right, now here's someone with an eye for quality! No cheap liquors for you, not a single drop. No sir, you're in it for the good stuff, the top-shelf, the real deal. You want a drink that'll go down smooth and speak to your sophi . . . sophist . . . sophisticuh . . . worldly tastes. One glass of Witt's Whiskey, coming right up! Huh? Yeah, that's my name, it's my drink, that's an assurance of quality! I'm a certified Legend. You think I'd slap my name on just any sponsored product? Come on, this is the official drink of the Paradise Lounge! Hm? Yeah, I own this place, too, what's your point?

YIELD
1 DRINK

COOK TIME
5 MINS

DIFFICULTY
BRONZE

INGREDIENTS

1 teaspoon absinthe
Handful of ice cubes
4 tablespoons rye or bourbon
1 teaspoon simple syrup
1 teaspoon maraschino cherry liqueur
¼ teaspoon Peychaud's bitters
¼ teaspoon Angostura bitters
Zest of 1 lemon

Additional equipment
Whiskey glass

PREPARATION

01. Add the absinthe to the whiskey glass and swirl so the inside of the glass is coated. (Among bartenders, this is known as rinsing.)

02. Add ice cubes to the glass.

03. Stir the whiskey, syrup, liqueur, and bitters in a small mixing cup and pour over the ice in the glass.

04. Rub the rim of the glass with lemon zest, then garnish with the zest and serve immediately.

THE NESSIE LATTE

I've learned that when people want to be friends with someone, they ask if that person would like to get a cup of coffee. I love making friends, so I decided I would try getting a cup, too! I can't taste it, though, so I'll give them mine as a gift. With so many different blends to try, I decided to start simple and go with this latte. Wattson loves Nessie, so surely she'll love Nessie's favorite drink, too! I'll have to share it with her after our next match, even though she's already my friend.

Wait, there's no coffee in this! I feel . . . deeply betrayed. And exhausted.

ARTIFICIAL ADVICE

Alternatively, you can use almond, oat, or rice milk for the foam topping instead of dairy milk.

YIELD
2 SERVINGS

COOK TIME
7 MINS

DIFFICULTY
BRONZE

INGREDIENTS

2 teaspoons matcha powder, plus more for garnish

⅞ cup hot water

1 tablespoon agave or maple syrup

⅔ cup milk

PREPARATION

01. Add the matcha powder to a mixing cup and cover with hot but not boiling water (ideally about 175°F). Use a small wire whisk or electric milk frother to beat thoroughly.

02. Add the syrup and stir well to combine. Divide the Nessie Latte into 2 glasses.

03. Heat the milk in a small pot over medium heat and beat thoroughly with the milk frother until foamy. Use a spoon to place a dollop of foam on the top of each glass. Sprinkle with additional matcha powder and serve immediately.

We've come to the end of our journey together. I'm doing all I can to savor that last bite before it's over—metaphorically. But the great thing about a book is that you can flip back to the first page and start the adventure all over again. I know I will once I finish writing this conclusion; I do have to edit it, after all!

I hope you've found some new favorite recipes in this book; I know I have, even though I can't eat them myself. As Catalyst would say, I was still able to "feed my spirit." I learned all sorts of new things about my fellow Legends and the places all over the Outlands. There can only be one winner in the Apex Games, but all of my friends are winners in this book. Winners at cooking and eating!

Absolutely, everyone's a winner, that's a great way to look at things, bud. Of course, you know, if you had to choose, my pork chops, like . . . they're the real winner, right?

Your pork chops get a gold star from me!

Uh, thanks, but that doesn't really answer my question.

And thanks to you, Mirage! I could not have written this book without you. Plus, with new players joining the Games and becoming Legends all the time, we may even be able to write another cookbook. That would be super fun!

And so much work, oof. But hey, maybe next time, we can work out a deal that's more moot . . . mutuaaa . . . mutually benefii . . . that actually gets us paid.

Don't worry. The Syndicate assured me that if this book is a success, they'll give us even more exposure next time!

Right . . . just going to flip back a few pages here because I need a drink.

Thanks again for reading, and remember, my new foodie friends: in the kitchen, you are the Champion!

CONVERSION CHARTS

VOLUME

U.S.	METRIC
⅕ teaspoon	1 ml
1 teaspoon	5 ml
1 tablespoon	15 ml
1 fluid ounce	30 ml
⅕ cup	50 ml
¼ cup	60 ml
⅓ cup	80 ml
½ cup	120 ml
⅔ cup	160 ml
¾ cup	180 ml
1 cup	240 ml
1 pint (2 cups)	480 ml
1 quart (4 cups)	1 l

TEMPERATURES

FAHRENHEIT	CELSIUS
200°	93.3°
212°	100 °
250°	120 °
275°	135 °
300°	150 °
325°	165 °
350°	177 °
400°	205 °
425°	220 °
450°	233 °
475°	245 °
500°	260°

WEIGHT

U.S.	METRIC
0.5 ounces	14 grams
1 ounces	28 grams
¼ pound	113 grams
⅓ pound	151 grams
½ pound	227 grams
1 pound	454 grams

Published by Titan Books, London, in 2023.

TITAN
BOOKS
A division of Titan Publishing Group Ltd
144 Southwark Street
London SE1 0UP
www.titanbooks.com

 Find us on Facebook: www.facebook.com/TitanBooks

Follow us on Twitter: @titanbooks

Published by arrangement with Insight Editions, San Rafael, California, in 2023. www.insighteditions.com

A CIP catalogue record for this title is available from the British Library.

ISBN: 9781803367026

Publisher: Raoul Goff
VP, Co-Publisher: Vanessa Lopez
VP, Creative: Chrissy Kwasnik
VP, Manufacturing: Alix Nicholaeff
VP, Group Managing Editor: Vicki Jaeger
Publishing Director: Mike Degler
Executive Editor: Jennifer Sims
Associate Editor: Sadie Lowry
Senior Production Editor: Michael Hylton
Production Associate: Deena Hashem
Senior Production Manager,
Subsidiary Rights: Lina s Palma-Tenema

Production Manager: Tom Grimm
Conception & Recipes: Tom Grimm
Text: Jordan Alsaqa
Photography: Tom Grimm & Dimitrie Harder
Typesetting, Cover & Layout: Dennis Winkler
Photo on page 146 ©Frank Parker/Adobe Stock

Apex Legends Narrative Team
David Bartle, Yonah Gerber, Sabrina Mah, and Ashley Reed

Additional Contributors
Manny Hagopian and Jaclyn Seto

Special Thanks to
The Respawn Art Team, Eduardo Agostini, Bilal Arshad, Tom Casiello, Roshni Damani, Amanda Doiron, Rosanne Elkington, Cristina Ferez, Sam Gill, Ryan Haaland, Christina Kim, Kevin Lee, Brett Marting, Ify Nwadiwe, Christal Rose Hazelton, Pete Scarborough, Molly Strongwater, Audrey Wojtowick, and Heather Woodward

Special thanks to Mela Lee for use of her personal family recipe for Lifeline's "Pas Me Dat Suga" Sugar Cookies—aka Mela's Miracle Cookies

Acknowledgments
Enrico Bongo, Ben Brinkman, Steve Ferreira, Evan Nikolich, Daniel Suarez, Greg Wilson, and Vince Zampella

Manufactured in China by Insight Editions

10 9 8 7 6 5 4 3 2 1